Silent Witness:

Quaker Meetinghouses in the Delaware Valley, 1695 to the Present

*Historic American Buildings Survey Recording
of Friends Meetinghouses within the Region of
Philadelphia Yearly Meeting*

ACKNOWLEDGEMENTS

The presentation of the Historic American Buildings Survey recording of Friends meetinghouses in the Delaware Valley is made possible by grants from the following organizations: The Marshall-Reynolds Foundation, the Anna H. and Elizabeth M. Chace Fund, Philadelphia Yearly Meeting Bequests Funds, The Historic American Buildings Survey/Historic American Engineering Record Foundation, Philadelphia Yearly Meeting Publications Grants Group, and the Thomas H. and Mary Williams Shoemaker Fund.

The catalog, and accompanying exhibition and symposium, were developed by the Philadelphia Yearly Meeting/Historic American Buildings Survey Working Group:
Clerk, Mather Lippincott, Cope & Lippincott Architects
William Bolger, Landmarks Coordinator, Philadelphia Support Office, National Park Service
Francis G. Brown, retired General Secretary, Philadelphia Yearly Meeting
Pam Carter, PYM Standing Committee of Support & Outreach
Paul M. Cope, Jr., Cope & Lippincott Architects
Christopher Densmore, Curator, Friends Historical Library of Swarthmore College
John Andrew Gallery, Clerk, Philadelphia Quarterly Meeting
Harold Jernigan, Clerk, Little Egg Harbor Monthly Meeting
Emma Lapsansky, Professor of History & Curator, Quaker Collection, Haverford College
Catherine Lavoie, Historian, Historic American Buildings Survey, National Park Service
Peggy Morscheck, Director, Quaker Information Center
Paul Rodebaugh, Historian & representative of Middletown Preparative Meeting
Sandra Sudofsky, Arch Street Meetinghouse

The initial exhibition of *Silent Witness* was hosted by The Athenæum of Philadelphia through the generous support of Dr. Roger W. Moss, Executive Director, and Bruce Laverty, Curator of Architectural Collections. The Athenæum is a member supported, not-for-profit, special collections library founded in 1814 to collect materials "connected with the history and antiquities of America, and the useful arts, and generally to disseminate useful knowledge" for public benefit. Located in a National Historic Landmark building near Independence Hall, The Athenaeum is operated as an historic site museum furnished with American fine and decorative arts from the first half of the nineteenth century. The Athenaeum offers diverse programs of public education, community outreach, lectures and changing exhibitions. For more information visit www.philaathenaeum.org.

Published by Philadelphia Yearly Meeting of the Religious Society of Friends with support and assistance of the Historic American Building Survey of the National Park Service and the Quaker Information Center.

ISBN 0-941 308-12-x

CONTENTS

Historic American Buildings Survey

The Historic American Buildings Survey of the National Park Service, Department of the Interior, was established in 1933 to create jobs for architects and photographers left jobless by the Great Depression. The greater mission of the program was then and is today to create a lasting archive of America's architectural heritage. In so doing, the HABS collection provides a database of primary source material for scholars, architects, preservationists, and students of history. As stated in the initial HABS proposal written by Charles E. Peterson, "The survey shall cover structures of all types from the smallest utilitarian structures to the largest and most monumental. Buildings of every description are to be included so that a complete picture of the culture of the times as reflected in the buildings of the period may be put on record." In 1934 the National Park Service entered into an agreement with the Library of Congress and the American Institute of Architects as cosponsors of the HABS program. Under this tripartite agreement the National Park Service administers the operations of HABS and sets qualitative standards. The Library of Congress preserves the records and makes them available to the public. The American Institute of Architects provides professional counsel. Since the 1950s, college students pursuing degrees in architecture, architectural history, and other related fields have undertaken recording with the guidance of trained project supervisors and the Washington, D.C., staff. Today, the HABS documentation is regarded as one of the nation's premiere architectural collections with records on over 28,000 buildings nationwide. For more information visit the website at http://www.cr.nps.gov/habshaer/habs/index.htm. This site also provides a link to the Library of Congress's *American Memory, Built in America* site where you can view the HABS collection online.

Philadelphia Yearly Meeting

When Quakers immigrated to the New World they brought with them an organizational structure that had only recently been developed in England. Three types of Friends meetings had been created, each named for the frequency with which it met for meetings for business and each covering a different geograhic area. The basic unit of the Society of Friends was, and still is, the monthly meeting so named because it constituted a group of Friends who met once a month to conduct meetings for business. Individual Quakers belong to monthly meetings. A number of monthly meetings in a given geographic region join together to form a quarterly meeting which, as the name suggests, meets four times a year for business. Quakers from several quarterly and monthly meetings in a larger geographic area meet once a year as a yearly meeting to discuss broad issues of the Society.

Quaker settlement in the Delaware Valley began in New Jersey, and by 1681 members of several monthly meetings formed a yearly meeting in Burlington. Rather than form a second yearly meeting, Pennsylvania Quakers joined the yearly meeting in Burlington forming what is now Philadelphia Yearly Meeting in 1685. Yearly meeting was held alternately at Burlington and in Philadelphia until 1760, after which time it was held only in Philadelphia. In 1827 differences within the Society of Friends led to a separation into two yearly meetings, both meeting in Philadelphia; they were reunited in 1955.

Today, Philadelphia Yearly Meeting (PYM) is an event, a faith community and an organization. As an event it is an annual time when Friends come together for a four- or five-day gathering for worship, fellowship, and to engage and enlarge Friends witness in the world. As a faith community PYM encompasses almost 12,000 people living in the eastern half of Pennsylvania, most of New Jersey, Delaware, and the eastern shore of Maryland. As an organization, PYM provides a variety of support services and resources to members, to 104 constituent monthly meetings, and to other Friends institutions. For more information visit the website at http:www.pym.org.

FRIENDS IN THE DELAWARE VALLEY

by Christopher Densmore

T he Society of Friends originated in Great Britain in the 1640s and 1650s, a period of religious and political turmoil. Quakers were one of a number of religious groups that challenged the authority of the Anglican Church. As dissenters from the dominant culture of the time, Quakers suffered persecution, fines and imprisonment in Britain until the Act of Toleration of 1689, and some legal restrictions against Friends in England were not lifted until the mid-19th century.

Traveling Friends reached the North American colonies in the mid-1650s, making converts among religious dissenters in New England, New York, Maryland, and Virginia. The first yearly meeting in North America was organized at Newport, Rhode Island, in 1671. In 1674, English Quaker proprietors purchased the territory of West Jersey, and Quaker settlements were begun at Salem in 1675 and at Burlington, in 1677. The success of the New Jersey ventures encouraged William Penn to form a colony of his own, and he subsequently obtained a charter for Pennsylvania in 1681.

The religious freedom and generous land policy Penn established for Pennsylvania attracted Quakers and other English, Welsh, Irish, and German settlers in large numbers. While many Quakers settled in Philadelphia, others spread out over the rich agricultural farmland of southeastern Pennsylvania quickly forming

both city and rural monthly meetings. Philadelphia became the hub of a major area of Quaker settlement, with local Quakers founding schools, hospitals, almshouses, and other institutions for the education and welfare of the population. Though a minority of the population, Quakers were the majority of the government of Pennsylvania, remaining so until 1756 when an unwillingness to appropriate funds for war with the Native Americans and a bounty on Indian scalps led most Quakers to withdraw from the Pennsylvania legislature.

Within the Society of Friends, Philadelphia Yearly Meeting was often considered the most influential of the yearly meetings outside of the original London Yearly Meeting. Though yearly meetings are independent of one another, Quakers on both sides of the Atlantic Ocean were tied together by the visits of Friends traveling in the ministry, by the epistles exchanged by the yearly meetings, and by a shared literature. A Friend in rural Pennsylvania in the 1750s might have more awareness of the developments within the Quaker community in New or old England than she would have of non-Quakers in

William Penn. (Friends Historical Library of Swarthmore College.)

the next county. Quakers were set apart from the wider culture by their many testimonies, notably their pacifism, and, by the mid-18th century, their opposition to slavery. Quaker testimonies on plainness were marked by plain dress, plain speech, and simple architecture.

Quakers in Pennsylvania were remarkably unified in belief and behavior during the 17th and 18th centuries. There had been a minor controversy with the followers of George Keith in the 1690s, and some Friends left the Society to fight for the American Revolution; a few of them formed the Free Quakers. In the early 1700s, the Quaker Reformation began a period of strict adherence to the discipline of the Society of Friends and a willingness to disown from membership those who deviated from the Quaker way by joining the military, attending "places of diversion," or marrying non-Quakers. In 1688, Friends in Germantown prepared a protest against slavery. Philadelphia Yearly Meeting advised its members against the slave trade as early as 1696, and by the 1750s, led by Quaker reformers, including John Woolman (1720–1772) of Mt. Holly (NJ), and Philadelphia educator Anthony Benezet (1713–1784), the yearly meeting voiced its condemnation of the practice of owning slaves. The final step came in 1776, when Philadelphia Yearly Meeting required that any Friend who did not accept the yearly meeting's admonition to liberate his or her slaves would be disowned.

The unity that marked 18th-century Quakers fragmented in the early 19th century. By 1820, disagreements among Friends about evangelical theology and the role of ministers and elders in the affairs of the Society led to factionalism. The sense of fragmentation may have been heightened by social and economic differences between urban and rural Friends. In 1827, Philadelphia Yearly Meeting divided into "Hicksite" and "Orthodox" branches, and the division traveled outward to all of the local meetings and beyond the

Lucretia Mott. (Friends Historical Library of Swarthmore College.)

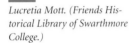

Abington (Hicksite) Meetinghouse. (Friends Historical Library of Swarthmore College.)

boundaries of Philadelphia Yearly Meeting to the other Quaker bodies in North America. In many places where one meeting had been, there would be two bodies both claiming to be part of the authentic Society of Friends. Generally the numerically stronger party retained the old meetinghouse, and the other side built a new one in the vicinity of the old meeting. The yearly meeting boarding school at Westtown remained in the hands of the Orthodox, while the Hicksites built George School. The Orthodox created Haverford College in 1833, and the Hicksites chartered Swarthmore College in 1864. To those outside the Society of Friends, there would be little in the appearance or lifestyle to distinguish the one side from the other. In the 1840s and 1850s, the Orthodox Friends were further divided into Wilburite/Conservative and Gurneyite/Evangelical camps, though within Philadelphia Yearly Meeting the division of sentiment did not result in an actual separation in the yearly meeting as it did elsewhere in North America. In the 1850s, some Hicksites left their branch of Philadelphia Yearly Meeting to form the Pennsylvania Yearly Meeting of Progressive Friends. The revival movement of the 1870s, strong among Midwestern, New York, and North Carolina Friends, had little impact in Philadelphia Yearly Meeting.

Quakers of the 18th and early 19th centuries tended to emphasize Friends' distinctiveness from the wider society, shown in visible ways by plain dress and the simple style of the meetinghouse, and in personal behavior by adherence to social testimonies of pacifism, temperance, and antislavery. In their own eyes Quakers were supposed to be a "peculiar"—meaning distinctive—people, and much concern was taken for the guarded education and upbringing of its members so they did not fall prey to the corrupt practices of the world's people. In the 19th century, some prominent Friends exemplified by James and Lucretia Mott, following the lead of Woolman and Benezet, felt that the proper application of Quaker testimonies concerning antislavery, peace, the equal treatment of women, and temperance required an active engagement in the world. Strict adherence to standards of dress was not important; active benevolence was.

By the later 19th century, Friends in both branches of Philadelphia were cooperating with each other on social issues. The establishment of American Friends Service Committee during World War I brought Hicksites and Orthodox, Wilburites and Gurneyites together in common causes. By 1920, and for some Friends well before, there was a growing feeling that the old divisions between Hicksite and Orthodox were not relevant to modern times. A gradual process of reuniting Quaker meetings, and cooperating in Quaker institutions, led to the final reunion of the two branches of Philadelphia Yearly Meeting in 1955.

No organization remains static. Despite the continuing influence among Friends of the example and writings of the first generation of Quakers, particularly George Fox, and on the later examples of John Woolman and Lucretia Mott, both of them members of Philadelphia Yearly Meeting, the interpretation of Quaker beliefs and testimonies changed over time. In the early 19th century, Quaker plainness was represented by a distinctive form of dress; by the 20th century, few Quakers wore such distinctive dress although most contemporary Quakers avoid ostentation and ornamentation in clothing. In much of the 18th and 19th century, Quaker testimonies, for many Friends, meant a clear separation from "the world," where for contemporary Friends those same testimonies require an active engagement in the world.

Historic American Buildings Survey Recording of Friends Meetinghouses within the Region of Philadelphia Yearly Meeting

by Catherine C. Lavoie

From the founding of the Religious Society of Friends in 1652 until the passage of the 1689 Act of Toleration, Friends in England were unable to worship openly without fear of reprisal. Consequently, the followers of George Fox, founder of the Quaker movement, had been forced to meet in houses, barns, and other buildings adapted for use as meeting places. Only rarely did English Friends attempt to build a structure for the explicit purpose of holding Quaker worship prior to the 1690s. Many traveling Quaker ministers preferred open-air meetings. And even once free to build meetinghouses, the practice of adapting cottages or other preexisting buildings often persisted. Friends began immigrating to New Jersey in the 1670s and to the Pennsylvania colony in 1681. The religious toleration guaranteed by William Penn in Pennsylvania permitted Friends the freedom to pursue their beliefs and to develop building forms conducive to their silent meeting for worship, and separate men's and women's business meetings. The variety of meetinghouse forms produced during the period of early settlement in the Delaware Valley speaks to both their freedom and the lack of prescribed standards for meetinghouse design. Early Quaker settlers adhered to a pattern for these meetings established in England that would inform the plan of their meetinghouses. However, given the autonomy to experiment with meeting practice as well as building design, the colonial Friends eventually deviated from English meeting practice. This only served to further facilitate the development of their own distinct building forms. American Friends meetinghouse designs continued to evolve over the course of time to adapt to changing patterns of Quaker faith and practice. Today over 150 meetinghouses historically associated with Philadelphia Yearly Meeting (PYM) still stand, several in near-original condition. Ranging in date from as early as 1695 to as late as the 1970s, they present an unparalleled opportunity to document the evolution of an important American building type.

Detail of window at the south front facade of Radnor Meetinghouse. (Jack E. Boucher, photographer, 1998.)

Despite the significance of the meetinghouse architecture in the PYM region and the availability of primary research materials located at repositories such as Swarthmore College's Friends Historical Library and Haverford College's Quaker Collection, very little has been written on the topic. Most interpreters of Quaker history have focused on the impact of Friends religious beliefs upon social ills, motivating Friends to effect change through good works and the establishment of reforming institutions. It was not until 1996 that Historic American Buildings Survey (HABS) of the National Park Service recognized that a comprehensive study was needed to identify and selectively record Friends meetinghouse architecture of this region and provide the context for its evaluation and interpretation. Beyond the academic usefulness, it was hoped that the study would create awareness of the historical and architectural value of meetinghouses and promote their preservation.

The information presented here represents the culmination of a multi-year effort undertaken by HABS to record the architecture of Friends meetinghouses within the Delaware Valley and its environs. The study encompassed the area under the care of PYM whose constituent meetings extend throughout eastern Pennsylvania, Delaware, and southern New Jersey. As the centers of Quaker religious and social life, the meetinghouses are crucial to the understanding of the Quaker experience and the importance placed upon community. As artifacts of the built environment, the meetinghouses serve as tangible reminders of the vast contributions of Friends to the history and development of the Delaware Valley. The meetinghouses are often well-preserved and so provide an important venue for studying the area's early vernacular architecture. But perhaps most intriguing, taken as a group, the meetinghouses survive as physical manifestations of the changing expressions of Quaker faith and practice over the course of three centuries.

The HABS study began with a field survey of Friends meetinghouses located within the greater Philadelphia area to include Bucks, Chester, Delaware, and Montgomery counties in Pennsylvania. The survey identified the essential elements of meetinghouses and, along with preliminary research, recorded historical data such as construction dates, accounts of prior meetinghouses on the site, and monthly/quarterly meeting associations. The survey located over eighty extant meetinghouses. The information was compiled

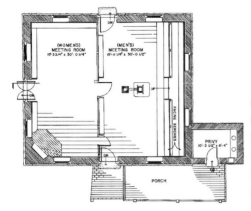

Of the meetinghouses in the Delaware Valley, the plan of Chichester Meetinghouse comes closest to that of English meetinghouses. However, its symmetrical, single-cell exterior was particular to colonial designs. (Adam Maksay, Kevin J. Lam, and Roger S. Miller, delineators, 1997.)

Drawing of the retractable wood paneled partition at Chichester Meetinghouse. The partition that divided the meetinghouse into separate men's and women's meeting rooms was an essential design feature. (Roger S. Miller, delineator, 1997.)

and examined both chronologically and by region or quarter to reveal specific types, periods, and patterns of meetinghouse development. Representative meetinghouse forms were then selected for HABS recording based upon architectural integrity and their ability to exemplify a particular stage in the evolution of Friends meetinghouse design from the earliest immigrations to modern times. In the summer of 1997, a field team of architectural technicians working under the direction of HABS architects, the survey historians, and the HABS photographer, produced measured drawings, written histories, and large format photographs of the first six meetinghouses, those of Merion (ca. 1695–1714), Radnor (1718), Buckingham (1768), Chichester (1769), Caln (1726, rebuilt 1782), and West Grove (1903).

HABS returned to the field during the Spring of 1999 to expand the scope of the survey. Recognizing that Quaker culture and the influence of PYM extended beyond Philadelphia and the counties immediately surrounding it, the second phase of the field survey included structures built by meetings in other areas of Pennsylvania, Delaware, and New Jersey. Altogether, approximately 150 meetinghouses were examined. With matching funds from the William Penn Foundation, a second team was fielded during the summer of 1999 for recording the meetinghouses at Sadsbury (ca. 1747), Frankford (1775), Arney's Mount (1775), Downingtown (1806), Little Egg Harbor (1863), Germantown (1869), Middletown (remodeled 1888), and Southampton (1969). In an effort to round out the selection, large-format photography and short historical reports were also prepared for Plymouth (1708), Old Kennett (ca. 1731), Bradford (1765), Roaring Creek (1796), Arch Street (1804), Darby (1805), Upper Providence (1828), New West Grove (1831), Abington Orthodox (1836), Race Street (1857), West Philadelphia (1901), Westtown (1923), and Chestnut Hill (1931) meetinghouses.[1]

Although Friends arriving in Pennsylvania in the 1680s brought with them no specific models of meetinghouse design, they did bring ideas about Quaker practice and about building traditions developed in England that would influence their approach to design. Like their English counterparts, colonial Quakers rejected the elaborate ornamentation and iconography of Anglican churches in favor of the plainness dictated by the tenet of simplicity. Therefore, it is less important to define meetinghouses in terms of prescribed architectural styles. Building *design* was more clearly driven by the use of indigenous materials and the vernacular building traditions that are responsible for the variations among meetinghouses in England and in America. Instead, *plan* played a more significant role in identifying particular meetinghouse types. Plan is essential to facilitating the meeting program. In fact, all major changes to Friends meetinghouse design over the course of their history coincide with changes in faith and practice. Among the practices that most influenced meetinghouse design were the business meetings and the designation of ministers, elders, and overseers.

Many colonial-era meetinghouse plans reflect the English pattern of meeting whereby men and women met together in a single room for meeting for worship and afterwards separated for business meetings, with the women's meeting held in another area. While the space allotted to the women's meeting sometimes was located in a loft or even in a separate structure, it was more often merely separated from the principal meeting room by a retractable paneled wood partition. Early on, Friends developed a system of ministers, elders, and later, overseers, to preside over the meeting for worship and attend to the affairs of the meeting. These individuals were seated in the tiered benches referred to as the "facing benches" ("the stand" or the "gallery") located in the principal meeting room. Thus facing benches and partitions became essential features of meetinghouses on both sides of the Atlantic.

In developing meetinghouses colonial Friends often began with a small log structure, none of the earliest of which survive. The earliest permanent meetinghouses in the Delaware Valley generally took one of two basic plans although they varied greatly in form and details. The first consisted of a roughly square-shaped structure containing back-to-back meeting rooms separated by a partition with a facing bench in the larger of the two rooms and a separate entrance into each room (see Sadsbury Meetinghouse and the plan of Chich-

---

[1] Delaware's Friends meetinghouses were not recorded as part of the current HABS project due to the efforts of students at the University of Delaware, under the direction of Professor Bernard Herman, who have undertaken measured drawings to HABS standards to be donated to the HABS collection. And while New Jersey's meetinghouses likewise appear to be underrepresented, many were recorded by HABS in the earlier days of the program.

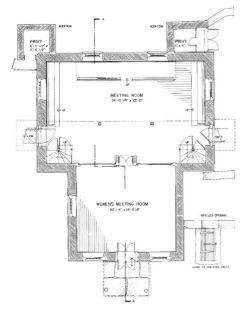

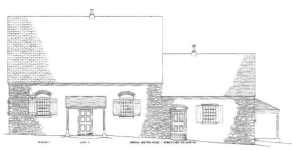

Plan of Merion Meetinghouse. Its T-shape and inequitable room arrangement reflects the lack of prescribed standards indicative of early colonial meetinghouse design. (Adam Maksay and Roger S. Miller, delineators, 1997.)

Drawing of south front elevation of the telescoping form of Radnor Meetinghouse. This form was created by the addition of a smaller women's meeting room to the earlier structure. (Roger S. Miller, H. Christie Barnard, and Adam Maksay, delineators, 1997.)

ester Meetinghouse). The second meetinghouse type consisted of a single-cell or one-room structure with an entryway to the center of the principal facade. In at least some cases, these single-cell structures were partitioned into two rooms of unequal proportions, but more often were left open as a single room. As the meeting grew in numbers, single-cell meetinghouses were enlarged to create additions subordinate to the larger structure and intended for use primarily by the women's meeting for business (see Radnor Meetinghouse). This additive quality later evolved into a two-cell meetinghouse with equal apartments for men's and women's business meetings (see Buckingham Meetinghouse).

By the late eighteenth century, Friends of PYM began meeting on both sides of a partition for worship *and* business, merely lowering the partition for the latter meetings. This meeting pattern called for a structure containing two rooms of equal proportions rather than one room large enough for the entire population and another only for the women. The new arrangement also required a facing bench in both rooms, which could best be achieved by placing the meeting rooms side-by-side and running the facing benches the length of the meetinghouse. The equally proportioned, two-cell meetinghouse constituted such a practical resolution in the quest for a building form conducive to both meetings for worship and business that it became the most prolific form in the Delaware Valley. Indeed, for nearly a century it was used as a prototype for the design of American Friends meetinghouses nationwide.

The two-cell plan would also appear in the return of the early single cell type that was selected by many of the new meetings that resulted from the 1827 schism that divided Friends into Hicksite and Orthodox contingents. Changes in faith and practice that grew out of the philosophical conflicts that precipitated the schism were also responsible for the introduction by some segments of the Quaker population of more mainstream ecclesiastical practices including the design of church-like meetinghouse forms. By the 20th century, programmatic changes such as the diminishing role of ministers, elders, and overseers, and a halt to the practice of holding separate men's and women's business meetings led to the elimination of the once-essential facing benches and partitions. Also by this time, other activities originally undertaken in separate buildings were combined within a single multi-use structure to include such elements as social room/library, schoolroom, kitchen, and restroom facilities.

In addition to the variations in meetinghouse design and/or plan, particularly among those structures erected during the first century of Quaker settlement, regional building traditions and materials also influenced meetinghouse design. During the HABS study it was observed that meetinghouses located within the same organizational unit of monthly or quarterly meetings shared common building traits, but often varied considerably from those of neighboring quarters. While the study attempts to outline an evolutionary process for the design of meetinghouses within the Delaware Valley, there are some variables worth noting. The PYM provided no guidelines for meetinghouse design or construction but instead allowed the individual meetings relative freedom to erect structures particular to their needs. This practice is reflected in the wide variety of meetinghouse designs that were produced. It was true even during the heyday of the two-cell prototype from the late 18th to the mid-19th centuries that some old designs persisted while newer ones were also being developed. Thus the evolution of meetinghouse design does not form a strictly linear progression, rather early patterns of development have a habit of reappearing (albeit in somewhat altered form). Also noteworthy is the fact that while many meetings either construct new meetinghouses or alter old ones to conform to new patterns of Quaker faith and practice, a significant number continue to use older, seemingly antiquated structures. This latter practice is important because it underscores one of the fundamental principles of Quaker worship; because it is free of ritual and sacrament it demands no set building form.

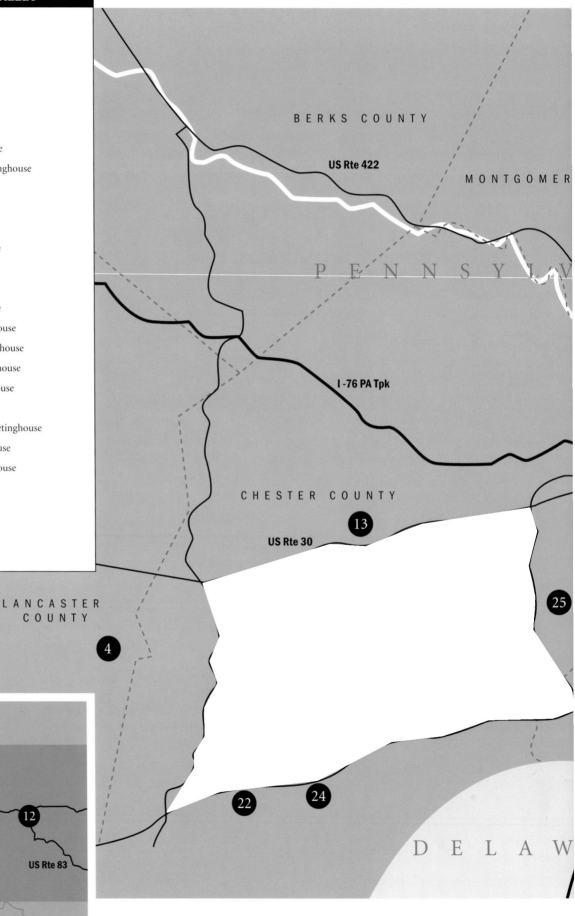

QUAKER MEETINGHOUSES IN THE DELAWARE VALLEY

1   Merion Meetinghouse

2   Radnor Meetinghouse

3   Plymouth Meetinghouse

4   Sadsbury Meetinghouse

5   Chichester Meetinghouse

6   Bradford Meetinghouse

7   Arney's Mount Meetinghouse

8   Frankford Preparative Meetinghouse

9   Buckingham Meetinghouse

10 Darby Meetinghouse

11 Old Kennett Meetinghouse

12 Roaring Creek Meetinghouse

13 Caln Meetinghouse

14 Arch Street Meetinghouse

15 Downingtown Meetinghouse

16 Upper Providence Meetinghouse

17 Abington Orthodox Meetinghouse

18 Race Street Friends Meetinghouse

19 Little Egg Harbor Meetinghouse

20 Germantown Meetinghouse

21 Middletown Preparative Meetinghouse

22 New West Grove Meetinghouse

23 West Philadelphia Meetinghouse

24 West Grove Meetinghouse

25 Westtown Meetinghouse

26 Chestnut Hill Meetinghouse

27 Southampton Meetinghouse

BERKS COUNTY

US Rte 422

MONTGOMER

PENNSYLV

I-76 PA Tpk

CHESTER COUNTY

13

US Rte 30

25

LANCASTER
COUNTY

4

22   24

DELAW

US Rte 80

PA   12

US Rte 83

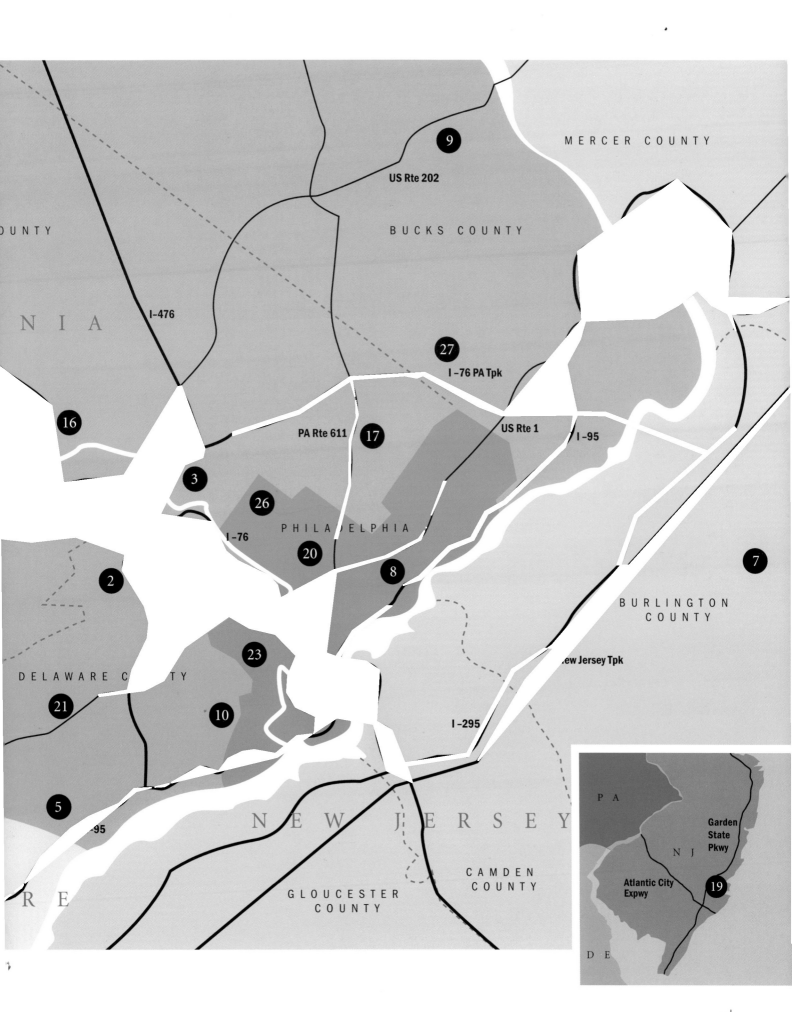

MERCER COUNTY

9

US Rte 202

BUCKS COUNTY

NIA

I-476

27

I-76 PA Tpk

16

PA Rte 611

17

US Rte 1

I-95

3

26

I-76

PHILADELPHIA

2

20

8

7

BURLINGTON COUNTY

23

New Jersey Tpk

DELAWARE COUNTY

21

10

I-295

5

NEW JERSEY

95

CAMDEN COUNTY

GLOUCESTER COUNTY

RE

PA

Garden State Pkwy

NJ

Atlantic City Expwy

19

DE

MERION MEETINGHOUSE (ca. 1695–1714)

(Lower Merion Friends Meetinghouse)

615 Montgomery Avenue at Meeting House Lane, Merion Station, Montgomery County,
Pennsylvania, HABS No. PA-145

Interior detail of early window frame east gable end. (Jack E. Boucher, photographer, 1997.)

In 1681, a delegation of Friends from North Wales petitioned William Penn for lands in his new colony of Pennsylvania, hoping to establish their own Welsh "Barony," or self-governing state. As the founding members of the Society of Friends in Wales, they constituted the first generation of Quaker converts. Among them were some of the builders of Merion Meetinghouse, the first of the Welsh Tract settlers to arrive. Referring to themselves as the "Merioneth Adventurers," in reference to their home village, they landed in Upland (Chester) in 1682, two months ahead of Penn's initial visit, and prior to the laying out of the city of Philadelphia. In addition to being among the pioneering Friends to put Penn's Holy Experiment into practice, they are also acclaimed as the first known migration of a Celtic-speaking Welsh community to the Western Hemisphere.[2] Their meetinghouse was one of the earliest meetinghouses erected in the Delaware Valley and among the few from the turn of the 18th century to survive. For over 300 years it has served as the center of religious and social life for the Friends of Lower Merion Township.

Meetings for worship among the Merion Friends were held initially in the homes of various members. The construction of their meetinghouse began as early as 1695 and was completed by 1715, making it the oldest extant Friends meetinghouse in the Delaware Valley. Its T-shaped near cruciform plan appears to be unprecedented in meetinghouse design and, therefore, has been the topic of some controversy.[3] Many resist the idea that persecuted emigrant Friends would adopt a plan so closely resembling one used by the Anglican Church when they rejected all that such a structure represented. It may be, however, that its seemingly unusual configuration reflects the lack of prescribed standards governing the design of meetinghouses erected by the earliest Quaker settlers to the Delaware Valley. Religious persecution, and their own belief in the unsuitability of "steeple-houses" for Quaker worship, discouraged the members of the Society of Friends in England and Wales from developing a meetinghouse building type prior to the 1689 Act of Toleration. Unfettered by the persecution experienced by their English counterparts, Friends who immigrated to the Delaware Valley beginning in the 1670s were free to create public meetinghouses. Lacking a prototype, Merion Friends may have looked to the rural parish churches of their homeland for architectural inspiration.

The T-shaped plan also appears unconventional by later Friends standards because it was not conducive to the American Friends practice of equal proportioning of space for men and women. Instead, the women's meeting section placed at the front of Merion Meetinghouse is smaller than the main room beyond it, where the tiered facing benches from which the ministers, elders, and overseers preside over the meeting for worship are located. Merion's plan, however, is indicative of the colonial Friends adherence to the English pattern of meeting whereby men and women met *together* for worship and afterwards separated for business meetings. Such an arrangement necessitated that the room used for women's business meetings be only about half the size of the principal meeting room used for worship and men's business, and it did not require facing benches. This arrangement allowed for far greater flexibility in meetinghouse plan.

Merion Meetinghouse is also of interest for its use of medieval English building traditions as seen in the stone construction, steeply pitched roof with timbers cut to resemble a cruck (naturally curved or bent member rising from the outer walls to support the roof), remnants of original leaded casement windows, pent eaves, and doorway hoods. Considering the primitive environment of the colony at the time in which Merion Meetinghouse was erected, the limited availability of skilled craftsmen, and the temporary nature of most early colonial era structures, Merion's sturdy construction and refined architectural elements surely must have set it apart. For the purposes of the HABS study, Merion's early and unpatterned design distinguishes it as the beginning point in the evolution of Friends meetinghouse design in the Delaware Valley.

Detail view of date stone in west gable end of meetinghouse. (Jack E. Boucher, photographer, 1997.)

---

[2] William Bolger, National Historic Landmark Nomination, Merion Friends Meetinghouse, Merion Station, Pennsylvania; prepared 1997.

[3] Samuel J. Bunting, "Merion Meeting House, 1695–1945; A Study of Evidence Relating to the Date" (Philadelphia: publisher unknown, 1945), 2.

South (front) elevation of meetinghouse. (Jack E. Boucher, photographer, 1997.)

Interior view from the former women's meeting room into the larger, principal meeting room, looking north through the partitions towards the facing benches. (Jack E. Boucher, photographer, 1997.)

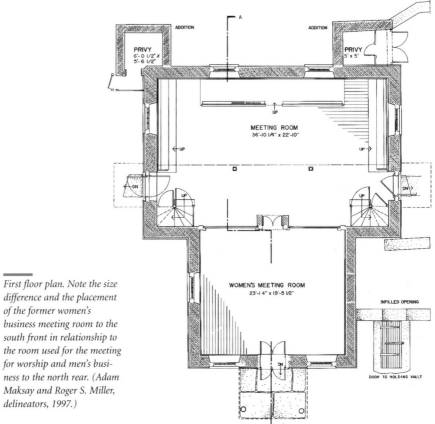

First floor plan. Note the size difference and the placement of the former women's business meeting room to the south front in relationship to the room used for the meeting for worship and men's business to the north rear. (Adam Maksay and Roger S. Miller, delineators, 1997.)

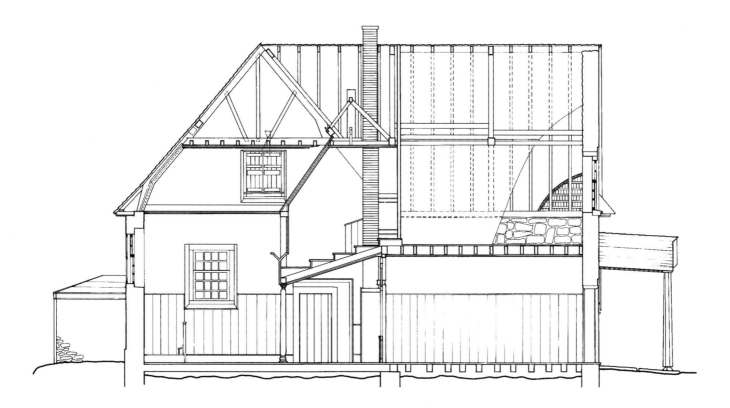

Longitudinal sectional drawing looking east to show meeting rooms, loft, and structural framing. Note the "cruck" timber and the location of the casement window in the gable end. (Adam Maksay and Roger S. Miller, delineators, 1997.)

View of raised clerk's desk located on the upper tier of the facing benches, north room, looking east. (Jack E. Boucher, photographer, 1997.)

RADNOR MEETINGHOUSE (1718)

SW corner of Conestoga & Sproul Roads, Ithan, Delaware County, Pennsylvania,
HABS NO. PA-6226

View of principal meeting room looking northeast towards the partition and, beyond it, the east meeting room. (Jack E. Boucher, photographer, 2000.)

The telescoping form of Radnor Meetinghouse reflects patterns of 18th-century Friends meeting-house development extant in perhaps no other structure in the Delaware Valley. As was typical of many rural 18th-century meetinghouses in the region, Radnor began in 1718 as a single-celled, three-bay-wide, center entry structure. The addition to the main building of a smaller, two-bay supplemental room used for women's business meetings and a school is reflective of the early attempts by the Society of Friends in America to develop a building form that best facilitated the greater needs of their community, as well as their unique form of worship and separate men's and women's business meetings. This building type likely evolved from the need to erect a meetinghouse for worship as soon as possible, with the idea that Friends would add a women's meeting section when they were better able, or perhaps when their numbers necessitated it. Preoccupied with establishing their own homes and farms, the Friends who first settled the colonies were often hard-pressed to contribute to the construction of a meetinghouse. From the standpoint of design and proportion, women's meeting additions such as Radnor's appear almost as separate structures, and in some cases were actually treated as such.

Like the Merion Friends, the earliest to settle in Radnor were among the first generation of Welsh Quaker converts. The first of the Friends from Radnorshire arrived with those from Merionethshire, in 1682, and two more families accompanied William Penn on his first trip to the colony shortly thereafter. An indulged meeting—or meeting for worship only—was established here in 1683. The Welsh Friends of Merion, Radnor, and Haverford comprised a monthly meeting and had hoped to establish their own barony within the newly formed Pennsylvania Colony. Elements of Radnor's meetinghouse, such as its steeply pitched roof, are indicative of medieval English building traditions. Meetinghouses such as Radnor were of Friends own design and construction, with individuals contributing according to their ability. Members of the meeting—generally elders or those with skill in the building trades—were appointed to oversee the various phases of construction, acting as a general contractor would today. Whenever possible, capable members would undertake the actual construction. According to the minutes for Radnor Meeting, "Some friends of those appointed to assist Radnor Friends in ye contrivance of a new meetinghouse there bring acct yt. They have accordingly mett and given ym their thoughts as to ye bigness and form thereof to wch (which) Radnor frds then there present seemed generally to agree with."[4] Statements such as this testify to communal nature of the design and construction process for meetinghouses. Friends within the meeting came together and were often joined by the larger monthly and/or quarterly meeting of which they were a part in order to build a new meetinghouse. The Radnor Meetinghouse remains in active use and, in fact, recently received a rear addition. Designed by Quaker architect Paul M. Cope, Jr., the addition is in keeping with the original structure.

Drawing of south front elevation. Note the telescoping form that includes a smaller section for women's business meetings at the east end. (Roger S. Miller, H. Christie Barnard, and Adam Maksay, delineators, 1997.)

Facing page: *Perspective view of west gable end. Note the steeply pitched roof that is indicative of the old English thatched roofs. (Jack E. Boucher, photographer.)*

[4] Radnor Monthly Meeting, Minutes, 14 day 9 mo 1717.

PLYMOUTH MEETINGHOUSE (ca. 1708; addition ca. 1780)

SW corner of Butler & Germantown Pikes, Plymouth Meeting, Montgomery County, Pennsylvania, HABS No. PA-6689

View under the porch of south front facade, looking west. (Jack E. Boucher, photographer, 1999.)

Plymouth Friends Meeting was formed as an indulged meeting for worship in 1702 by members of Haverford (later Radnor) Monthly Meeting as a meeting of convenience during times of severe weather. As stated in the minutes, "The representatives of Harferd (sic.) Monthly Meeting laid before this meeting, that some friends belonging to their meeting living att and near Plymouth being so far from them desired that they may have a first days meeting for [the] service of Truth to be held during this winter time, to which this meeting agrees and desires that frds [friends] may remember to visit them."[5] By the following winter, the Plymouth Friends requested that their indulged meeting be established as a "settled meeting" to which the quarterly meeting agreed.[6] The first meetings were held in the homes of members Hugh Jones and David Meredith, until the current meetinghouse could be built, sometime between 1708 and 1714.[7]

Plymouth Meetinghouse is indicative of the practice of expanding or otherwise altering early meetinghouses to meet later programmatic changes. Much like Radnor Meetinghouse, Plymouth began as single-cell building, and by the late 18th century received a smaller, telescoping structure to be used for the women's business meetings. Following a fire that necessitated the partial reconstruction of the meetinghouse, the current eastern section—previously referred to in the minutes as the "little meetinghouse"— was rebuilt in a manner that was more in keeping with the design and proportions of the main block.[8] The new section maintains the same roof line and is separated by a retractable wood partition rather than by a wall, as had previously been the case. Plymouth Meeting remains active, and the site has been expanded to include a school complex, parts of which are housed in rehabilitated carriage sheds.

View of interior of the original section of the meetinghouse. Note the somewhat unusual placement of the gallery in the gable end only. (Jack E. Boucher, photographer, 1999.)

---

[5] Philadelphia Quarterly Meeting, minutes, 7 day 10 mo 1702.

[6] Ibid., 7 day 4 mo 1703.

[7] Pennsylvania Historical Survey, Division of Community Service Programs, Work Projects Administration. *Inventory of Church Archives, Society of Friends in Pennsylvania* (Philadelphia: Friends Historical Association, 1941), 142.

[8] Plymouth Preparative Meeting minutes, 4 day 9 mo. 1806.

SADSBURY MEETINGHOUSE (1747)

Simmontown Road 2 miles E of Rte. 41, Christiana vicinity, Lancaster County, Pennsylvania, HABS No. PA-6651

Detail of typical window, southeast elevation. (Jack E. Boucher, photographer, 1999.)

Sadsbury Meeting was established in 1724 by the New Garden Monthly Meeting and consisted of Friends migrating westward from the Philadelphia area. In the following year, a log meetinghouse was erected. By 1737, the meeting was elevated to monthly meeting status and over the next decades would continue to maintain a strong presence in the area. Sadsbury Meeting grew to become the largest monthly meeting in Caln Quarter and was responsible for setting up most of the meetings that surround it. In keeping with the increasing size and influence of Sadsbury Meeting, a more substantial stone meetinghouse was built in 1747 upon land granted to the trustees of Sadsbury Meeting by the colony's proprietors, William Penn's sons Thomas and Richard.

View from east meeting room looking through the open partition into the west meeting room and out the southwest doorway. (Jack E. Boucher, photographer, 1999.)

The meetinghouse stands today as a rare extant example of an early meetinghouse form. This square-shaped, hipped-roof type included centrally located entries on the southeast and southwest elevations, in effect, creating two contiguous front facades. Sadsbury resembles those meetinghouses built in late 17th and early-18th-century Philadelphia, such as the 1703 Second Bank Meetinghouse. Like the Second Bank Meetinghouse, Sadsbury's square configuration and dual entries reflected the positioning of the room created for women's business meetings to the rear of the principal room that contained the facing benches and that was used for men's business and joint meetings for worship. The partition at Sadsbury is likely in its original location, to the westerly side of the central doorway located on the southeast facade that provided entry into the principal apartment. The doorway at the southwest facade provided entry into the smaller apartment behind it that was used for women's business meetings. The relationship between these rooms was one that was conducive to the English pattern of meetings and was used in numerous other Delaware Valley

Perspective view of the southwest and southeast facades that provide separate entryways into the men's and women's rooms. The finer stone coursing and the beltcourse between the two stories on the southwest facade suggests that it was intended as the principal facade. (Jack E. Boucher, photographer, 2000.)

meetinghouses from the late-17th to mid-18th century. The facing benches originally located along the northeast wall were later relocated to the northwest wall, and the gallery that once opened onto them (running along the southeast, southwest, and northwest walls) was destroyed in a fire. Evidence of the original plan, however, is found in the attic space where the outline of the former gallery is clearly visible.

At the turn of the 20th century, Sadsbury Friends decided to abandon the old meetinghouse and build a more modern structure in town. The structure begun in 1902 was a vast departure from the 1747 meetinghouse. Instead of the traditional open space divided by a partition with the facing benches as its focus, the new meetinghouse contained a full church-like plan including a narthex or entrance hall, central aisle, and an organ. By 1920 Friends found the more modern arrangement unsatisfactory and resolved to once again have all the "overseers, elders, and others at the head of [the] meeting sit facing the meeting," an arrangement they felt added "dignity, strength, and inspiration" to the meeting.[9] In 1973, Friends of Sadsbury Meeting chose to return to the 1747 meetinghouse which was renovated for that purpose. The 1902 structure was then sold to the trustees of the Christiana Mennonite Church.[10] Friends continue to meet in the historic meetinghouse.

Sectional drawing looking northwest. Note the remnants of the former gallery that opened onto the northeast wall; the break in the gallery indicates the previous location of a stairway. (Irina Madlina Ienulescu and James McGrath, Jr., delineators, 1999).

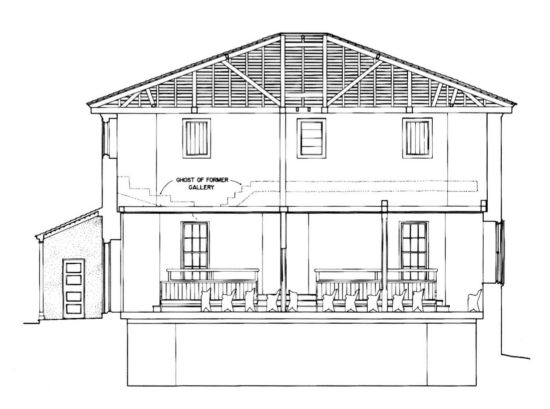

GHOST OF FORMER GALLERY

9 Sadsbury Preparative Meeting, joint minutes 1917–1925, 4 day 1 mo. 1920, p. 22.
10 Virginia Price, "Sadsbury Friends Meeting House," National Park Service, Historic American Buildings Survey, HABS NO. PA-6651, Summer 1999. Price, Sadsbury Friends Meetinghouse (Christiana), HABS NO. PA-6675.

CHICHESTER MEETINGHOUSE (1769)

611 Meetinghouse Road, Upper Chichester Township, Delaware County, Pennsylvania,

HABS NO. PA-6225

East gable end of meeting-house. (Jack E. Boucher, photographer, 2001.)

The area in which Chichester Meetinghouse is situated was the scene of some of the earliest Quaker settlement in the Pennsylvania Colony. Before Pennsylvania was founded Friends settled in what was then referred to as West Jersey, in areas such as Burlington and Salem. Some migrated across the Delaware River and established meetings prior to William Penn's arrival. Among them was Robert Wade, who migrated to Upland (Chester) as early as 1675 from an earlier Quaker settlement located in West Jersey. Other Friends did the same, establishing meetings at Shackamaxon (Kensington), Tacony (Frankford), and The Falls (Fallsington). Wade began a meeting for worship in his new home, which functioned as an indulged meeting of the Burlington, New Jersey, Monthly Meeting from which these early Friends originated. Quaker settlement in this area continued to grow. In 1681, Wade's meeting was recognized as the Uplands Monthly Meeting (renamed Chester in 1711). As a monthly meeting, the Upland Meeting was empowered with the ability to establish other meetings. One of these was Chichester Meeting, created as an indulged meeting in 1682, the same year that William Penn arrived with other Friends to form the Pennsylvania Colony. Meetings were then held in member homes as was the custom, particularly in the case of an indulged meeting intended for worship only. In 1687, Chichester Meeting declared their intent to erect a stone meetinghouse 24-feet-square in plan. The next year a grant of two acres from fellow Quaker James Browne was made for that purpose. This structure stood until January 1769, when it was consumed by fire. The extent to which the newly constructed meetinghouse, begun that same year, differed from the original is not known. Although its size increased to approximately 33' x 38', it still maintained a configuration that was basically square in shape. The new meetinghouse also incorporated a plan that remained consistent with older meeting patterns.

North elevation of meeting-house. (Jack E. Boucher, photographer, 2001.)

The current Chichester Meetinghouse is a well-preserved and unusual example of 18th-century Quaker meetinghouse architecture. It is the best extant illustration of a meetinghouse with a layout that represents an interpretation of English meeting patterns and meetinghouse plans. Although not erected until 1769, Chichester's plan is reflective of an earlier period. It was among the last meetinghouses in the Delaware Valley to follow such a plan, one that the emerging American Friends forms would soon prove outmoded. At Chichester, the facing bench is located in one gable end with a double-door entry in the opposing end (and single entrances to the center of both side elevations). Similar to the plan of Merion and the original plan of Sadsbury, Chichester's designers partitioned the building in such a way as to exclude the facing bench from one of the two meeting rooms. Unlike English meetinghouses, however, the distinct interior spaces created for men's and women's business meetings are given no exterior expression. Instead, the exterior mirrored the central-entry, single-cell configuration that was typical of many early settlement period meetinghouses in the Delaware Valley.[11]

Like most Quaker builders, the Friends who erected Chichester Meetinghouse drew from local vernacular building traditions. The meetinghouse demonstrates how local interpretations of the Quaker tenet for simplicity or Plain Style left room for refinement, exhibiting distinctive features such as a decorative water table that highlights corners and doors, a corner fireplace, an early iron stove, and a secondary, waist-high partition door. Chichester Meeting was "laid down" or discontinued many years ago, and the meetinghouse is now used only for special events. For this reason, the Friends saw no need to alter the meetinghouse or to add modern conveniences such as plumbing and electricity and so the building remains in near pristine condition.

Wood stove that heats the east room of the meetinghouse. (Jack E. Boucher, photographer, 2001.)

Below: *Plan of meetinghouse. Note that facing benches are located in the east room only, which is indicative of English patterns of meeting. (Adam Maksay, Kevin J. Lam, and Roger S. Miller, delineators, 1997.)*

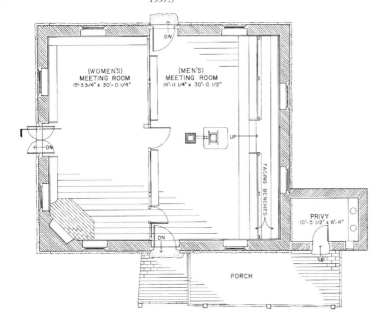

Corner fireplace and bench in the west room, formerly the women's meeting room. (Jack E. Boucher, photographer, 2001.)

---

[11] Aaron Wunsch, "Chichester Friends Meeting House," National Park Service, Historic American Buildings Survey, HABS NO. PA-6225, Summer 1997.

BRADFORD MEETINGHOUSE (1767)

(Marshallton Friends Meetinghouse)
1364 West Strasburg Road, Marshallton, Chester County, Pennsylvania, HABS No. PA-1105

Structural framing in attic, looking southwest. (Jack E. Boucher, photographer, 1999.)

In 1716, an indulged meeting was set up in Marshallton, Bradford Township during the winter months only for the convenience of a gathering of Friends from the Kennett Meeting living further up the Brandywine River and not wishing to travel the distance in inclement weather. In 1726, a "settled" or year-round meeting was officially established by Newark Monthly Meeting and a log meetinghouse was erected. By about 1729 a more substantial stone meetinghouse was built, and the log building was converted for use as a stable. Construction on the current meetinghouse began as early as 1765. By 1767, the new meetinghouse was ready for use and in 1768 the earlier structure was dismantled and its parts sold.[12]

View from the west meeting room through the open doors of the partition into the mirror-image east meeting room. This view speaks to the equal rooms created for men's and women's meetings by the late 18th century. (Jack E. Boucher, photographer, 1999.)

---

[12] Western Quarterly Meeting minutes, 17 day 8 mo. 1767. Bradford Preparative Meeting minutes, 10 day 6 mo. 1768, and 11 day 10 mo. 1768.

As was common practice among Friends, members of a building committee developed a design and saw to the construction of the meetinghouse. Bradford's vernacular character is reflected in its simplistic treatment of finish elements, its fairly diminutive scale, and the use of indigenous stone as a building material. In keeping with Quaker plain styling, rubble work was favored over a more decorative pattern of cut stone or ashlar. However, the precision stonework and fine galleting or infill of stone fragments exhibited at Bradford Meetinghouse are the marks of a highly skilled mason. The masonry may, in fact, be the work of weighty or influential Bradford Friend and noted colonial botanist Humphrey Marshall who served on the building committee for the meetinghouse. Marshall fashioned the stonework of his own house in much the same manner as seen at Bradford. Both structures also included an unusual internal flue system. The system was later abandoned in the meetinghouse but is still visible from the attic. If Marshall is responsible for the design the lack of credit given to him can be said to be in keeping with the communal nature of the Quaker design and construction process, and the reluctance to single out any one person's contributions.

Like Chichester Meetinghouse, Bradford's *original* plan more closely followed that of a typical English meetinghouse. When built in 1767, Bradford's interior plan consisted of a larger room and facing bench at one end, partitioned off from a smaller secondary room for women's business meetings. The plan was later changed to conform to new patterns of meeting program that became popular during the late 18th century, and the partition was relocated to run north-to-south rather than east-to-west. The changes to the interior configuration of the meetinghouse likely occurred following a 1788 fire originating from the stove that had been lit early that morning to warm the meetinghouse prior to the First-day (Sunday) meeting. The floor still bears the marks from the fallen embers.[13]

Among the interesting features of Bradford Meetinghouse is an unusual partitioned section located along the front of the meetinghouse, the original intent of which is unknown. It has been suggested that the shallow section created by the lowering of this partition was used to cordon-off certain individuals, such as slaves or other nonmember observers, or perhaps mothers with young children who might disrupt the meeting. Glazed panels in the partition allow light from the windows in the south elevation to pass through to the principal meeting space, but their height would not permit seated individuals a view into the room. It is more likely that the partition enabled the building to conform to the size of a smaller meeting (such as a preparative versus a monthly meeting) thereby conserving heat while facilitating the sense of a close-knit community. Bradford Meetinghouse is also of interest for its near original condition. Although it is still in use, it has received no modern additions or renovations, and is still without central heat, electricity, and plumbing.

[13] Bradford Preparative Meeting minutes, 6 day 3 mo. 1788.

Arney's Mount Meetinghouse (1775–1776)

(Mount, or Shreve's Mount, Friends Meetinghouse)

SW corner of Juliustown & Pemberton-Arney's Mount Roads, Springfield Township,
Burlington County, New Jersey, HABS NO. NJ-1243

View from east side of gallery looking through the doorway into the west side. Note the open shutters to the north that overlook the principal meeting room on the first floor. (Jack E. Boucher, photographer, 2001.)

Arney's Mount, also known as Shreve's Mount or simply Mount Meeting, was set up under the care of Burlington Monthly Meeting, in 1743. Located in rural southern New Jersey, the Friends held their early meetings in an old schoolhouse. The current two-story, single-cell meetinghouse is a vernacular structure constructed of local Bog Iron stone, in 1775–1776. Arney's Mount Meetinghouse is the best extant example of this regionally specific Friends meetinghouse form, and it is one of a handful of meetinghouses within Philadelphia Yearly Meeting to remain almost completely unaltered from the time of its construction in the 18th century. Its fairly diminutive size and scale of other elements such as its windows, doorways, and entry porches exemplifies the tendency of Friends meetinghouses to more closely resemble domestic rather than ecclesiastical building forms. Furthermore, its use of indigenous materials and restrained detailing are indicative of the Quaker plain style of meetinghouse design.

Arney's Mount was part of a boom in meetinghouse construction that occurred within Burlington Quarter in 1775 and 1776. Four new meetinghouses were built, three of which were (then) part of the Burlington Monthly Meeting, including Mt. Holly, "Shreves" Mount, and Springfield or Copany. Of these, Arney's Mount Meetinghouse is the only example of its type to remain intact. (Copany, for example, was

View of the east side elevation. Note the open doorway that corresponds to a doorway in the same location in the west elevation. (Jack E. Boucher, photographer, 2001.)

altered for use as a residence). Among the identifying features of the Arney's Mount type is lack of an interior partition that traditionally separated concurrent men's and women's business meetings. Instead, a shuttered gallery may have served to fulfill that function until 1850, when the meeting no longer found it necessary to conduct business meetings separately.[14] Although much of the interior likely dates to the reconstruction that followed a (second) fire in 1811, the facing benches, gallery, and other wood elements and finishes are intact. The development of this meetinghouse form may have been influenced by meeting size, it being all that was necessary to accommodate a small, rural Quaker community. The relative freedom given to the individual meetings by Philadelphia Yearly Meeting to design and construct meetinghouses particular to their needs is demonstrated through the occurrence of regional specific forms such as Arney's Mount Meetinghouse. Coupled with the still rural nature of the surrounding landscape, the Arney's Mount Meetinghouse of today is almost indistinguishable from that portrayed in historic photographs. The building is still being used by Friends as a meetinghouse, although it's without electricity and plumbing; and a wood stove serves as the only heat source.

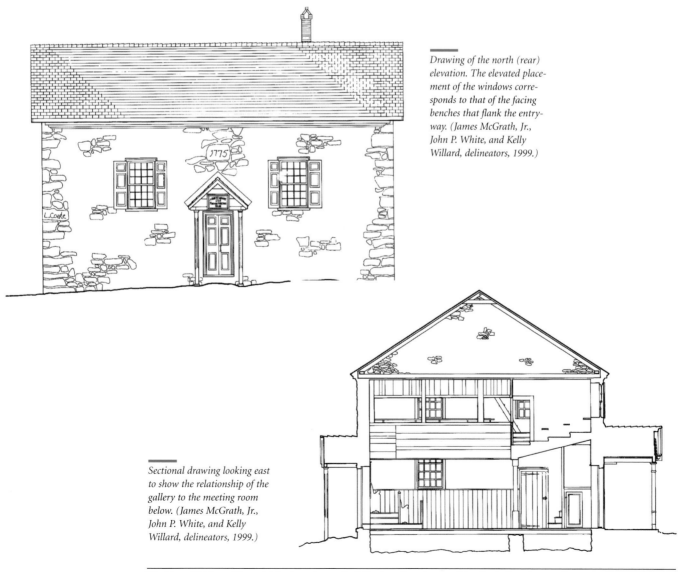

Drawing of the north (rear) elevation. The elevated placement of the windows corresponds to that of the facing benches that flank the entryway. (James McGrath, Jr., John P. White, and Kelly Willard, delineators, 1999.)

Sectional drawing looking east to show the relationship of the gallery to the meeting room below. (James McGrath, Jr., John P. White, and Kelly Willard, delineators, 1999.)

---

[14] In (Arney's) Mount Women's Meeting minutes, the following minute is entered (no date) after minute 27day 10 mo 1847: "After 2 mo. 1850, Men's and Women's Preparative Meetings at the Mount were united and held as one meeting—(signed) Barclay White."

FRANKFORD PREPARATIVE MEETINGHOUSE (1775–1776; addition 1811–1812)

4371 Waln Street at Unity Street, Philadelphia, Pennsylvania, HABS NO. PA-6652

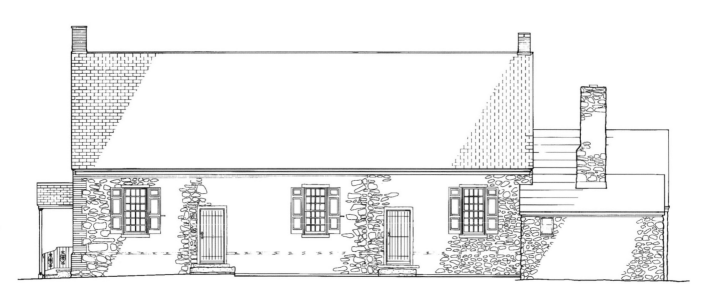

Drawing of south front elevation. Note the seam in the stonework to the side of the east doorway that indicates the location of the 1811–1812 addition. (Elaine Schweitzer and John P. White, delineators, 1999.)

Top right: *Detail shows the joining of the Flemish-bond brick west facade with the rubble-stone south facade. The brick was reused from the earlier meetinghouse. (Jack E. Boucher, photographer, 2000.)*

Frankford Preparative Meeting (now called Unity Meeting, Frankford) is among the oldest Friends meetings in the Philadelphia region. Its roots can be traced to the establishment of one of the first meetings in the Pennsylvania Colony, originating in the home of Thomas Fairman at Shacka-maxon prior to the coming of William Penn. Upon his arrival, Penn directed Fairman to relocate and establish a new meeting at Tacony in Oxford Township, later renamed Frankford. The current Frankford Preparative Friends Meetinghouse replaced the original ca. 1702 brick meetinghouse. The main block was erected in 1775–1776, making it the oldest standing Friends meetinghouse in Philadelphia. Although the construction of meetinghouses within the city dates back to its founding in the 1680s, most were replaced by the 19th century and some more than once. Frankford Meetinghouse began as a single-cell, three-bay, center-entry structure. Evidence indicates that a partition located to the east of the central doorway once divided the 1775–1776 meetinghouse into two unequally sized apartments. In 1811–1812, this meeting pattern was manifested in the external appearance of the building through the addition of a two-bay section that would better accommodate the women's business meetings. In both cases, the smaller size of the eastern (women's) apartment suggests a meeting pattern established by the English whereby Friends met in a single room for worship, and then in separate apartments for men's and women's business meetings. Frankford reflects a critical point in the evolution of meetinghouse design in which the smaller additions for women's meetings became better integrated with the main block, and are not seen as a separate and/or telescoping structure. The partition has since been removed.

Frankford Meetinghouse is also of interest for its unusual mix of building materials. A refined treatment of Flemish-bond brick with glazed headers was used in constructing those facades facing the street including the western end where a single formal entry is located. The use of locally quarried rubble stone gives a more vernacular appearance to the remaining south front and east end facades. The utilization of both brick and stone was probably as much a function of economy as fashion; the bricks from the previous meetinghouse were reused and supplemented with stone. Such building practices were indicative of Quaker thrift whereby salvaged materials found new life in another structure or were otherwise put to good use.

The meetinghouse was retained by the Hicksite Friends following the 1827 schism and the Orthodox Friends met in private houses until a meetinghouse could be built nearby at the corner of Orthodox and Penn streets in 1832. Membership decreased during the first decades of the twentieth century and the meeting was laid down or discontinued in 1928. The meeting was later revived, and in 1947 and 1962, a restroom, and kitchen and class rooms additions, respectively, were made to the meetinghouse. Membership continued to wane, but the meeting has been renewed recently and in spring of 1999 was reinstated as Unity Meeting, Frankford.

BUCKINGHAM MEETINGHOUSE (1768)

5684 York Road, Lahaska, Bucks County, Pennsylvania, HABS NO. PA-6224

Top right: *Detail of typical window, south front elevation. Note the wood bar used to hold the shutters open. (Jack E. Boucher, photographer, 1999.)*

Above: *Perspective view of the south front and west side facades. Note the equal proportioning of the meetinghouse, and the gabled hoods over the dual entryways. (Jack E. Boucher, photographer, 1999.)*

By the last quarter of the 18th century, a new meetinghouse form emerged that would set the standard for meetinghouse design for the next century. Built in 1768, Buckingham Friends Meetinghouse is the earliest known example of the two-cell, symmetrically balanced or *doubled* type that became a conventional form for American Friends meetinghouses. While prior meetinghouse forms usually consisted of either a three-bay-wide building partitioned to create unequally sized apartments, or a telescoping form with distinct sections for men's and women's business meetings, the Buckingham Meetinghouse was unique in that it treated the two sections as equal parts of a whole structure. More importantly, the design expressed a programmatic change. Although American Friends continued to maintain close contact with their English counterparts, transformations were occurring in the colonies centered on the treatment of the women's business meeting. In contrast to the early style of meeting, men and women now sat on separate sides of the partition for worship *and* business, merely closing the partition during the latter meetings. Thus, Buckingham combined a new meeting program with a design based upon the duplication of the original single-celled unit as exemplified by the main blocks of Radnor and Frankford meetinghouses.

Above left: *Detail of timber-framed king-post truss system that supports the roof framing, looking northeast. (Jack E. Boucher, photographer, 1999.)*

The standardization of meetinghouse design represented by the proliferation of the Buckingham type coincided with important events in Quaker history such as that of a spiritual reform movement resulting in the further rejection of mainstream society. An influential segment of the Society believed that a complacency had fallen on later generations of birthright Friends resulting in a weakening of the Discipline or rules governing conduct. A rise in affluence and involvement in worldly affairs were cited as key factors in the decline. As a means for reviving the deep spiritual inwardness that characterized the earlier period a call went out for stricter adherence to Friends doctrine.[15] Through the leadership of Philadelphia Yearly Meeting, Quaker discipline was rewritten and more attention given to the newly amended "queries" or questions to be answered regarding the state of the Society and the behavior of its members. Significantly, among the offenses to the discipline most frequently recorded in the minutes was "marrying out of meeting." Viewed as a threat to the purity of the Society, and thus, to Friends values, marrying a non-Friend was officially declared grounds for disownment in 1762. Because marriage issues fell under the purview of the women's meeting, the 1762 enactment appears to have significantly elevated the importance of the role of women within the meeting. While the reform movement was responsible for codifying rules and procedures that led to meetinghouse standardization, it also helped to balance the roles played by men and women, and it was likely responsible for the creation of equal apartments.

The current Buckingham Friends Meetinghouse is the fourth at this location. The meeting was established by Friends migrating from Falls Meeting which was among the first meetings in the Pennsylvania Colony. The first house was erected of logs between 1705 and 1708 and was located in the area of the (preexisting) burying ground. A wood frame meetinghouse was built next. Located a short distance from the southwest corner of the present meetinghouse is a single-story, one-bay, 22' square stone structure that is likely the remnant of the 1720 women's meeting addition to the second meetinghouse. A mounting or "upping block", used to facilitate the mounting and dismounting of horses, sits near this structure and is a further indication of its former use as a meetinghouse. A second mounting block is found to the west of the present meetinghouse, along the abandoned roadbed that served as a drive from York Road (originally located to the rear of the meetinghouse). Now sitting alone, this mounting block may likewise indicate the site of the third meetinghouse constructed of stone, ca. 1731. Finally, a mounting block is located to the northeast corner of the 1768 meetinghouse, near the former women's meeting section. In 1798 the stone schoolhouse that forms the nucleus of the current Buckingham Friends School was erected to the east of the meetinghouse. For nearly 300 years, this site has served as the focal point for the religious, social, and educational activities of Buckingham Friends.

Sectional drawing looking west. (Pamela Howell, delineator, 1997.)

[15] Howard H. Brinton, *Friends For 300 Years: The History and Beliefs of the Society of Friends Since George Fox Started the Quaker Movement* (Wallingford, Pa: Pendle Hill Publications, 1952), 176.

DARBY MEETINGHOUSE (1805)

1017 Main Street, Darby, Delaware County, Pennsylvania, HABS No. PA-6690

Stairway to gallery and built-in benches located in the southwest corner. (Jack E. Boucher, photographer, 2000.)

The founding members of Darby Meeting arrived in 1682 and established an indulged meeting for worship in the home of John Blunston that is mentioned in a letter from William Penn to Friends in England.[16] Darby was set up as a monthly meeting by Chester Quarterly Meeting in 1684. In 1687 the first meetinghouse was erected. This structure also served as Darby's town hall and was therefore a focus of activities for both the Quaker and non-Quaker communities. In 1701, a new meetinghouse was erected near the site of the first. Built in 1805, the current meetinghouse was located two blocks from the original site, and its large size testified to the growing strength of the Friends community in the area. The meetinghouse was designed in the two-cell form established with the construction of the Buckingham Meetinghouse that allowed for equal apartments for men and women separated by a retractable wood partition. Thus, Darby is significant as a good representation of the many meetinghouses that were constructed from the late-18th through the mid-19th century to replace older, seemingly antiquated designs. The meetinghouse includes significant intact architectural features and appears largely unaltered from its original design. One noteworthy exception is the porch that currently extends the length of the front elevation. Like many older meetinghouses, beginning in the 1860s, the traditional gabled doorway hoods were replaced by porches that provided social space for gatherings before and after meetings as well as protection from inclement weather. Interior features of interest at Darby Meetinghouse include the fireplaces, and the tiered benches built into the front and side walls of the meetinghouse that offset the elevated facing benches along the rear wall. The meetinghouse retains an active meeting.

South gable end of the meetinghouse. (Jack E. Boucher, photographer, 2000.)

[16] Letter dated 17th day 1st mo. 1683.

OLD KENNETT MEETINGHOUSE (ca. 1731)

U.S. Rte. 1, One mile N of Longwood Gardens, Kennett Square vicinity, Chester County, Pennsylvania, HABS No. PA-6230

Top right: *Detail of remnants of the fireplace and chimney in attic, looking northeast. (Jack E. Boucher, photographer, 2000.)*

Above: *Windows and principle entry, southeast front facade. Note that the partition that divides the meetinghouse into two rooms is mounted on a post that separates the paired doorways. (Jack E. Boucher, photographer, 2000.)*

Kennett Preparative Meeting was set up in 1711 by Newark Monthly Meeting. The establishment of Kennett and Centre Meetings marked the beginning of what would later become Western Quarterly Meeting (1758); they were the first meetings located beyond the Brandywine River to be established by Friends, some of whom arrived with William Penn in 1682. Old Kennett Meetinghouse was erected ca. 1731. Its single-cell, central-entry exterior appearance followed a meetinghouse plan that was typical of the early settlement period. At some later date, however, the window and doorway openings and roof were altered and the interior of the meetinghouse was reconfigured. The partition was likely moved from a position to one side of the doorway to its current location at the center of the meetinghouse where it is somewhat awkwardly mounted on a narrow post that separates the double doors of the front entry. These and other modifications were made in the effort to adapt an early building to the changing American Friends practice and were part of a larger pattern of alterations to meetinghouses in the Delaware Valley that began during the late 18th century. A central partition accommodated the equally sized apartments for men's and women's business that were indicative of meetinghouse forms of the late 18th and 19th centuries. Despite some reconfiguration, the meetinghouse is of exceptional overall integrity and includes many noteworthy features of 18th-century meetinghouse architecture including pegged floors, paneled partitions, elevated facing benches, and somewhat primitive turned posts and carved newels. The attic was originally finished as usable space and remnants of its former gambrel roof, fireplace heat, plastered walls, and built-in benches are still apparent. The meetinghouse has been largely unused for the past century and remains in a rustic condition, without central heating, plumbing, or electricity.

ROARING CREEK MEETINGHOUSE (1795)

Meeting Road off Rte. 42, Numidia, Columbia County, Pennsylvania, HABS No. PA-6691

Detail of door hardware. (Jack E. Boucher, photographer, 2001.)

In 1775 and 1786 Exeter Monthly Meeting in Berks County set up Catawissa and Roaring Creek Meetings respectively as indulged meetings located on what was then the Pennsylvania frontier. A preparative meeting was established at Roaring Creek in 1796, following the completion of the meetinghouse. Built in 1795, Roaring Creek Meetinghouse is of interest for both its log construction and its unequally proportioned two-cell design.[17] It is a single-story, dual entry structure built of hewn logs, with chinking and corner boards. Although many early-settlement-period meetinghouses were constructed of logs, they were viewed as temporary structures and were quickly replaced. This and the meetinghouse at nearby Catawissa are the only ones historically associated with Philadelphia Yearly Meeting built of logs that are still standing.

The interior of Roaring Creek Meetinghouse is primitive with unpainted plank-covered walls, plain wood facing benches, and a retractable partition. It is divided by the partition into two apartments of unequal size and varying architectural treatment, with the larger western apartment constituting three of the four bays of the facade. The principal entry is to the center of the west section; it is flanked by windows and has an opposing carriage door to the rear. The eastern section has only a single door to the front, with a window opposing it to the rear. The unequally sized apartments were indicative of the English pattern of meetings and reflected a plan that was not generally found in American meetinghouse designs of this period. Although the meetinghouse was erected during a single building campaign, the two sections are dissimilar in style, harking back to a time when women's meeting sections were treated as separate structures. Roaring Creek Meetinghouse's rustic construction and outmoded plan may be a consequence of its frontier location, then among the furthest outreaches of Philadelphia Yearly Meeting. The meetinghouse is currently owned by the township, but an annual meeting of Friends is held in June.

South front elevation. The larger western meeting room includes the doorway flanked by windows to the left; the smaller room to the east is indicted by a single doorway. (Jack E. Boucher, photographer, 2001.)

---

[17] Philadelphia Quarterly Meeting minutes, 8 mo. 1795.

CALN MEETINGHOUSE (built 1726; rebuilt 1784; addition 1801)

King's Highway at Meeting House Road, Thorndale, Chester County, Pennsylvania,
HABS No. PA-6227

A meeting at Caln dates to as early as 1713 when Friends Aaron and John Mendenhall first settled here. In the spring of 1715, Friends made application to the Concord Monthly Meeting for the establishment of an indulged meeting. By 1716, they were acknowledged as a preparative meeting by the quarterly meeting which stated that: The request of the Friends of the Inhabitance of Caln for a first Day's meeting to be Settled amongst them being Considered, it is the sense of this meeting that they may keep a first Day's meeting there and have liberty to Build a meetinghouse on the Land of John Mendinhall (sic.) according to the Friends' proposal.[18] A log meetinghouse was then built that would serve the Friends for the next decade. By that time a shift in the local Friends population encouraged the members of Caln Meeting to settle upon the current location just on the other side of the valley. A more permanent stone meetinghouse was built on the new site in 1726.[19]

---

[18] Chester Quarterly Meeting, minutes, 6 day 6 mo. 1716.
[19] Virginia Price, "Caln Friends Meeting House," National Park Service, Historic American Buildings Survey, HABS NO. PA-6227, Summer 1999.

As it appears currently, Caln Meetinghouse's design was influenced by the need to accommodate a quarterly meeting. In 1800, Caln and other Friends meetings in the area joined together under the auspices of Caln Quarterly Meeting. It was formed from parts of Chester and Western quarterly meetings that had grown too large to manage effectively and thus reflected significant increases in the Quaker population of this region. To accommodate gatherings of this larger organizational unit, constituent meetings sponsored a major addition to Caln Meetinghouse in the following year. Caln Friends chose to expand their meeting space by adding onto their existing meetinghouse in a manner that essentially mirrored its original six-bay form. But while the original section was divided inside by a central partition, the 1801 quarterly meeting addition contained a single open room. This arrangement visually represents the chain of meetings within Friends structure. Caln Meetinghouse, therefore, is uniquely suited to the interpretation of the Quaker system of preparative, monthly, and quarterly meetings that was crucial to the spiritual, financial, and organizational support of the Society. After the 1827 schism between Hicksite and Orthodox Quakers, this architectural arrangement took on a new significance. Both groups continued to meet in the building, a highly unusual circumstance made possible in part by the meetinghouse's generous proportions and linear disposition of rooms. Orthodox Friends continued to meet at Caln Meetinghouse until 1905. By then the local Quaker population had shifted to Coatesville, where a new meetinghouse was erected in 1911. Although the meetinghouse was being used only infrequently after that time, it seems that the meeting was never officially discontinued. When the Orthodox and Hicksite Friends of Caln Quarterly Meeting were reunited in 1952, the event was held at the Old Caln Meetinghouse. While the lack of central heat restricts its use, the summer quarterly meeting is still held at Caln.[20]

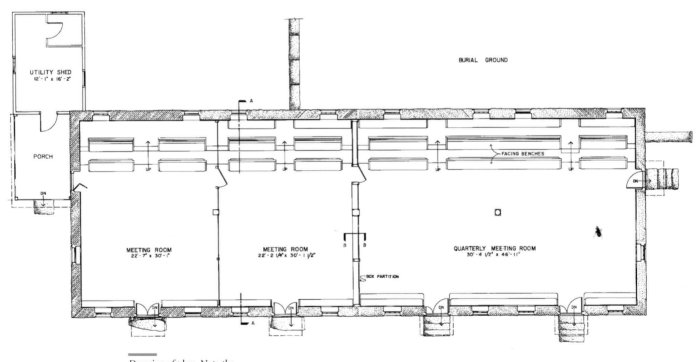

Drawing of plan. Note the original preparative meetinghouse on the left side and the open quarterly meeting addition to the right. (Kevin J. Lem, delineator, 1997.)

---

[20] Francis G. Brown, *Old Caln Meeting House: Its Story* (Glenmoore,Pa: Glenmoore Corporation, 2001), 28.

ARCH STREET MEETINGHOUSE (1804; 1811)

320 Arch Street, Philadelphia, Pennsylvania, HABS No. PA-1388

Stoop and boot scrape at entryway. (Joseph Elliott, photographer, 1999.)

Perspective view of the north (front) facade with entryways into the lobby and the flanking east and west meeting rooms. (Joseph Elliott, photographer, 1999.)

Philadelphia Yearly Meeting of the Religious Society of Friends was established in 1685 and was housed in a number of earlier meetinghouses prior to the construction of the current building. In 1804, the east wing and center section of the Arch Street Meetinghouse were erected according to a design developed by Quaker carpenter/architect Owen Biddle. The annual session of the women's yearly meeting was held here for the first time in 1804. The west wing was added in 1811, at which time the men's meeting was moved to the east section, and the women moved to the newly completed western section. Arch Street Meetinghouse is a symmetrically balanced three-part structure built of Flemish-bond brick. The center pavilion has a gable-front roof and entry portico and is flanked by two five-bay sections with a low-hipped roof and like portico. It is elegantly understated and therefore, despite its Georgian architectural styling and refined construction, is in keeping with Quaker plainness.

The impetus for the construction of the building is said to have come from the women of the yearly meeting, who wanted to accommodate the men's and women's yearly meetings in a single structure, as opposed to the use of separate meetinghouses as had occurred in the past. The completed meetinghouse contained a central hall and committee room flanked by identical meeting rooms. As such, the Arch Street Meetinghouse stands as a reaffirmation of the commitment to supporting both men's and women's meetings for business as established by the first yearly meeting of Delaware Valley Friends held in Burlington in 1681. George Fox, who founded the Society of Friends in England in the 1650s, advocated separate meetings for men and women as a means for insuring active participation by women in Quaker proceedings. In practice, the women's business meeting dealt primarily with social concerns such as marriage and aid to the needy while the men's meeting considered issues of policy and finance. Despite this fact, the attempt to place women on a par with their male counterparts was a radical one for its day and reflects a social consciousness indicative of Quaker beliefs. In contrast, unlike their colonial counterparts, English Friends did not consistently hold women's meetings for business. This factor is believed to have contributed to the development in the Delaware Valley of the two-cell meetinghouse that contains equal rooms for men's and women's meetings for business, a building form that does not appear in England.

Since 1811, the meetings of Philadelphia Yearly Meeting and the Monthly Meeting of Friends of Philadelphia have been held at Arch Street Meetinghouse. The original monthly meeting had grown so large by 1772 that it was divided into the Northern and Southern district meetings, to which was added a Western District Meeting in 1814, each with its own meetinghouse. Following the schism that divided Friends into Orthodox and Hicksite branches, this structure remained the yearly meetinghouse of the Orthodox Friends. After the reunification of the two branches of Friends meetings in 1955, Arch Street Meetinghouse continued to be used as the site of the annual sessions for Philadelphia Yearly Meeting.[21] Today it also serves as a conference center and museum; the restored West Room provides the site for yearly meeting sessions while the East Room is now a multipurpose facility.

View from the gallery looking southwest across the west meeting room. (Joseph Elliott, photographer, 1999.)

21 Virginia Price, "Addendum to: Arch Street Friends Meeting House," National Park Service, Historic American Buildings Survey, HABS NO. PA-1388, Summer 1999.

DOWNINGTOWN MEETINGHOUSE (1806)

800 East Lancaster Avenue, Downingtown, Chester County, Pennsylvania,
HABS No. PA-6653

Detail of wrought iron shutter stays on west elevation window. (Jack E. Boucher, 2002.)

Downingtown Meeting was established as an indulged meeting under the care of Uwchlan Monthly Meeting in 1806, at which time two acres of land were given to Friends on which to build a meetinghouse and plot a burying ground. However, as early as 1784 Friends in this area were allowed infrequent meetings which were held primarily during the summer months in an old Quaker schoolhouse. For the most part, prior to 1806 Downingtown Friends had to travel to the Uwchlan Meetinghouse in the village of Lionville about five miles to the north, or the equally distant Caln Meetinghouse to the west.[22] In 1811, Downingtown was recognized as a preparative meeting with the authority to hold meetings for business as well as worship. The meetinghouse is reminiscent of the single-cell building type developed by the Friends during the colonial period, which, by this time, had been largely supplanted by the doubled type. While the plan fulfilled the American Friends spatial requirements for two equally-sized rooms, the partition's orientation produced an interior arrangement indicative of earlier patterns. The partition extends from side to side running the length of the building. By the time of Downingtown's construction, common practice among Friends favored partitions that ran the width of the building with the facing benches open onto both apartments. Thus, Downingtown's arrangement was seemingly more conducive to English practice wherein men and women Friends met together for worship. The construction of Downingtown Meetinghouse, then, signaled a reemergence of earlier building forms in meetinghouse design. Its retrospective single-cell type characterized many of the meetinghouses that would be erected after the schism between Orthodox and Hicksite Friends in 1827. The single-cell or one-room plan was a viable solution because it easily accommodated the relatively small number of members in the new meetings created as a result of the separation, just as it had the small groups of immigrants a hundred years or so before.[23] Downingtown Meeting remains active, and the site includes a schoolhouse built in 1921 and currently used for social gatherings and other meeting functions.

North front elevation. (Jack E. Boucher, photographer, 2002.)

Sectional and corresponding northwest elevation drawings. (Elaine Schweitzer and Irina Madalina Ienulesca, delineators, 1999.)

---

[22] Francis G. Brown, *Downingtown Friends Meeting* (Glenmoore,Pa: Glenmoore Corporation, 1999), 2.
[23] Virginia Price, "Downingtown Friends Meeting House," National Park Service, Historic American Buildings Survey, HABS NO. PA-6653, Summer 1999.

UPPER PROVIDENCE MEETINGHOUSE (1828)

8207 Black Rock Road, Oaks, Montgomery County, Pennsylvania, HABS No. PA-6706

Built in 1828, Upper Providence Meetinghouse replaced the original log structure built in 1730 to serve an indulged meeting for worship. The current meetinghouse is of interest for its high level of architectural integrity, particularly with regard to its interior finishes. Like Downingtown Meetinghouse before it, Upper Providence also reflects the revival of the early single-cell form. The design of Upper Providence Meetinghouse includes even the long-abandoned rear carriage (or mounting) door. But like the later double-type meetinghouse, this structure is divided equally at its width. A partition is mounted on the post that separates the double doors of its front and rear entryways, belying the meetinghouse's single-cell exterior appearance. The resurgence of old building types or building elements demonstrates that the evolution of meetinghouse design does not always follow a linear progression—or more to the point—that old traditions are not easily forgotten. The meetinghouse exhibits noteworthy interior features such as stoves for heat, a barrel-vaulted ceiling, and tiered benches positioned along the east, south, and west walls that offset the elevated facing benches located along the north wall. It is also interesting to note the variations in bench designs particularly with regard to the profile of the bench ends, and it has been suggested that some benches came from the earlier meetinghouse on this site. The unusually high level of integrity demonstrated by Upper Providence Meetinghouse can be in part attributed to the fact that the meeting has been laid down for well over a hundred years and is now used by Friends only for special occasions. Without a meeting to make use of the structure on a regular basis, there was no need to update the interior furnishings or to install modern systems.

Top right: *Perspective view of east front facade. (Jack E. Boucher, photographer, 2000.)*

Above: *Detail of doorway that shows the partition mounted on the post between the doors, combining a single-cell exterior with a two-cell interior space. (Jack E. Boucher, photographer, 2000.)*

Interior view of meetinghouse looking northeast. Note the vaulted ceiling and built-in benches along all the walls, as well as the still rustic nature of the interior. (Jack E. Boucher, photographer, 2000.)

ABINGTON ORTHODOX MEETINGHOUSE (1836)

Jenkintown Road across from Fisher Road, Jenkintown, Montgomery County, Pennsylvania,
HABS No. PA-6657

Entryway at the south front elevation, looking northwest. (Jack E. Boucher, photographer, 1999.)

A s with Upper Providence, this meetinghouse combines a single-cell exterior with the interior configuration of the doubled prototype established by the construction of Buckingham Meetinghouse in 1768. Built in 1836, like many of its type, Abington Orthodox Meetinghouse was erected following the schism that divided Friends of the Delaware Valley and elsewhere into Orthodox and Hicksite branches, an event that occurred within Philadelphia Yearly Meeting in 1827. The split caused a boom in meetinghouse construction as the minority group left to form its own meeting. In this case, the Friends responsible for the formation of the meeting had withdrawn from the old and influential Abington Meeting in whose structure the quarterly meetings for this region were held. The Hicksite Friends were in the majority at Abington Meeting, and so the much smaller group of Orthodox sympathizers was obliged to leave the meeting in September 1827. They met in the home of Daniel Fletcher prior to the construction of this structure, sometimes referred to as "Little Abington" Meetinghouse. Abandoned and currently in a deteriorating condition, it is one of the few post-schism, Orthodox-built meetinghouses within Philadelphia Yearly Meeting that have not been altered for use as something other than a meetinghouse. It is currently owned by Abington Township, Parks and Recreation.

Interior of abandoned meeting room, looking east. (Jack E. Boucher, photographer, 1999.)

Race Street Meetinghouse (1856–1857)

Race Street W of 15th Street, Philadelphia, Pennsylvania, HABS No. PA-6687

Top right: *Stairway looking southwest. (Joseph Elliott, photographer, 1999).*

Left: *Race Street (north) elevation. (Joseph Elliott, photographer, 1999).*

Race Street Meetinghouse was erected in 1856–1857 to accommodate the yearly meetings of Hicksite Friends. Although erected almost 30 years after the ca. 1827 schism that separated the Friends of Philadelphia Yearly Meeting into Hicksite and Orthodox groups, the meetinghouse is a tangible reminder of the controversy caused by differing interpretations of Quaker doctrine in the early 19th century. Like its Orthodox counterpart located at Arch Street, Race Street Meetinghouse exhibits the refinement of a more urbane, brick-constructed building. The meetinghouse has matching facades on both Race and Cherry Streets, although the Race Street facade is considered the formal entrance. It is differentiated by the date stone placed in its gable end, and by its courtyard setback. Both facades are seven bays across and include three entryways that are protected by an overhanging entablature. The roof is gable-fronted and forms a broad pediment graced by an elliptical light. The interior of the meetinghouse consists principally of two large auditorium-style meeting rooms, 36 feet in height, separated by a wide stair hall. The northern room was designed to accommodate Philadelphia Monthly Meeting and the annual proceedings of the Women's Yearly Meeting of Hicksite Friends, while the smaller southern room was intended for use by the Men's Yearly Meeting. The meetinghouse also includes five committee meeting rooms.

The decision to begin construction on the Race Street Friends Meetinghouse was made in 1855 in response to a request by the women's meeting for safer, more comfortable, and more spacious quarters. As had occurred prior to the construction of the Arch Street Meetinghouse, before this structure was erected Hicksite Friends met in various other meetinghouses throughout the city, often with the men's and women's meetings forced to meet in separate buildings due to lack of adequate space. Begun in 1856, Race Street

Meetinghouse was completed by 1857 in time for the annual meeting of the Philadelphia Hicksites. In 1926, the men's and women's meetings were united and the southern room was turned over for use as a social hall. Race Street Meetinghouse remained the site of the Hicksite Philadelphia Yearly Meeting until 1955. It was then that Friends of Philadelphia Yearly Meeting were reunited at the Arch Street Meetinghouse.[24]

In 1975, the northern meeting room was restored and at the same time an addition was made to accommodate Friends Center. Together with the former Friends Central School building, these adjoining structures house the administrative offices of Philadelphia Yearly Meeting, American Friends Service Committee, and the Quaker Information Center. In 1992, Race Street Meetinghouse was designated as a National Historic Landmark for its associations with the Hicksite Yearly Meeting and it's recognition of women as active participants in their proceedings, for its role in supporting women's suffrage, and for the work of specific members such as abolitionist and women's rights activist Lucretia Mott and peace activist Hannah Clothier Hull. In addition to its administrative and business functions, Race Street Meetinghouse is currently being used by Central Philadelphia Monthly Meeting, an entity that resulted from the merger of the former Twelfth Street Meeting with Fifteenth Street Meeting.

Interior of north meeting room, looking northeast. (Joseph Elliott, photographer, 1999).

[24] Virginia Price, "Race Street Friends Meeting House," National Park Service, Historic American Buildings Survey, HABS NO. PA-6687, Summer 1999.

LITTLE EGG HARBOR MEETINGHOUSE (1863)

East Main Street, W of North Green Street, Tuckerton, Ocean County, New Jersey,
HABS NO. NJ-1118

Detail of the mechanism for lifting the partition. (Jack E. Boucher, photographer, 2001.)

Interior view from the west meeting room looking northeast through the open partitions into the east meeting room. (Jack E. Boucher, photographer, 2001.)

Edward Andrews was responsible for establishing a Friends meeting at Little Egg Harbor, as well as providing the lot upon which the first meetinghouse was erected. Andrews (along with his brother) came to this area from Upper Burlington County in 1702. He established a farm and built a grist mill on the property. This was among the first settlements in this area of the New Jersey colony and due to his influence, the town was originally referred to as "Quakertown" or "Andrews Mills." The first meetings for worship were held as early as 1702, probably in Edward Andrews's home, although an officially indulged meeting under the care of Chesterfield Monthly Meeting was not established here until 1709. In 1708, Andrews deeded two acres of his property to Friends on which to erect a meetinghouse and establish a burying ground. As an indication of Friends commitment to their faith, they had begun construction of a meetinghouse that year. The current meetinghouse bears little resemblance to the seemingly antiquated ca. 1709 structure that it replaced. A drawing made prior to its removal indicates that the earlier meetinghouse was a single-cell, shingle frame building with a gambrel roof to which was later appended a smaller gable-roof addition to accommodate separate women's business meetings.

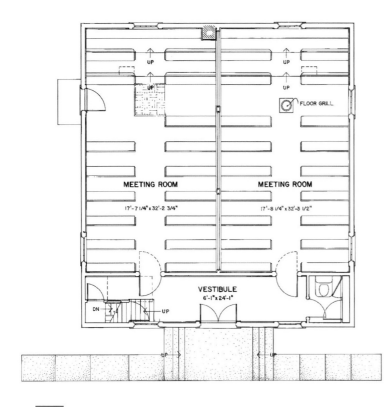

Drawing of plan. (Irina Madalina Ienulesca and John P. White, delineators, 1999.)

Erected in 1863, the design of Little Egg Harbor Meetinghouse reflects a later 19th-century trend within some (largely Orthodox) Friends meetings to adopt elements of mainstream ecclesiastical architecture. For this reason, it more closely resembles a small rural church than the typical Friends meetinghouse of the era. Little Egg Harbor's rectangular, gable-front configuration typifies the Greek Revival church design that was adopted almost universally by religious denominations from the 1820s through the 1860s. A period of extensive church building, spurred by westward migration and evangelical fervor, the Greek Revival church proved to be a prolific form. While most Friends meetinghouses at that time consisted of a two-celled structure with separate men's and women's entries positioned along the length of the building, Little Egg Harbor's meetinghouse has a single entry in the gable end with the facing bench on the opposite wall. Still, the meetinghouse is without ornamentation, remaining true to the Quaker tenet of simplicity. In addition, its plan includes a front lobby that provides for individual entrances into the men's and women's apartments, separated by the retractable wood partition that was traditional. The elaborate mechanism for lifting that partition, located in the attic, is among the most intriguing features of the structure. The meetinghouse is still actively used by Friends.

Perspective view of south front and east side facades. (Jack E. Boucher, photographer, 2001.)

GERMANTOWN MEETINGHOUSE (1867–1869)

47 West Coulter Street, Philadelphia, Pennsylvania, HABS NO. PA-6654

PENN' ANNO GER
OLD 1705 MAN
NEW 1812. TOWN

RE-BUILT
1869

Detail drawing of date stone which is a compilation of the date stones for all three meetinghouses to appear on this site. (Irina Madalina Ienulesca, Elaine Schweitzer and Kelly Willard, delineators, 1999.)

Germantown is a fine example of a mid-19th-century, urban meetinghouse. It was built in 1867–1869 by Quaker master builder Hibberd Yarnall and designed by Addison Hutton, one of Philadelphia's most accomplished Quaker architects. The commission was awarded to the firm of Sloan & Hutton just as Addison Hutton was in the process of dissolving his partnership with Samuel Sloan, under whom he had apprenticed. This structure is thus one of Hutton's earliest independent works, and it is likely the only Friends meetinghouse he designed. The meetinghouse maintains an austerity commensurate with the Quaker tenet of simplicity. However, it also exhibits elements of the high-style Italianate villas planned by well-known architects of the period, including Sloan & Hutton, for the city's rising class of businessmen and industrialists. Such elements include a broad wrap-around porch, large ornamental brackets, over-sized windows, and neatly-stuccoed exterior finish.

The design of Germantown meetinghouse also marks a significant shift in layout. Instead of a partition in the center of the room to accommodate separate men's and women's business meetings, as was typical of Friends meetinghouse design, the Germantown plan combines a main meeting room for worship and women's business with a rear Committee Room for the men's business meeting. The plan also deviated from the prototypical design by running the facing benches the width, not the length, of the building. Without a partition or gallery, the main meeting room is almost churchlike in its spaciousness and orientation. This distinctive, architect-designed meetinghouse reflected the rising affluence of Germantown Friends, just as its location foretold of the upcoming shift in Quaker demographics. By the late 19th century, Germantown was a center of elite Quaker society, and, at a time when many meetings were in decline, it was growing significantly. Although the Society of Friends had maintained a meetinghouse in Germantown since 1690, the new members were part of a migration of affluent urbanites who fled the increasingly congested city of Philadelphia for the quiet of the developing suburban neighborhoods. Suburban development in Germantown was facilitated by the establishment of one of the first commuter railroad lines.

Southeast front elevation. (Jack E. Boucher, photographer, 2000.)

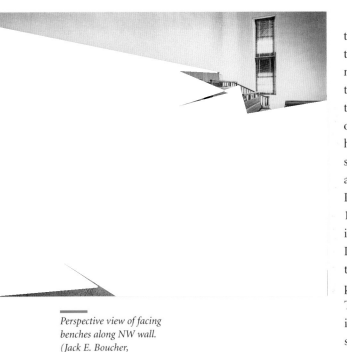

Perspective view of facing benches along NW wall. (Jack E. Boucher, photographer, 2000.)

In keeping with the isolationist tendencies of the Wilburite leaning Orthodox, Germantown Friends created a self-sufficient enclave of Quaker culture here by the mid to late 19th century. In addition to an innovative new meetinghouse, there were other improvements directed towards the preservation of their "peculiar" way of life. Perhaps most significant were new facilities to provide for the "guarded education" of Quaker children. The establishment of a Friends school was seen as important to the preservation of the Society; it helped to shield the next generation from the detrimental influences of the outside world, while indoctrinating it into the Quaker value system. In 1869–1870, a new structure was erected for Germantown Friends School, started in 1845. In 1873–1875, the Friends Free Library & Reading Room, also started in the 1840s, was given a new building. Although the library was open to non-Friends, it contained volumes carefully selected so as to be conducive to Quaker values. In terms of social life, the meetinghouse became the focus of a number of activities by the late-19th century. In 1889, the Committee Room benches were replaced with chairs, presumably to facilitate its use as a multipurpose room.[25] The kitchen and dining room, later referred to as the Social Room, were added in 1902 to accommodate among other events the well-attended "Tea Meetings" sponsored by the ladies of Germantown meeting. A meeting office designed by architect Richard A. Yarnall, grandson of the original builder, was added to the rear of the building in the 1960s.

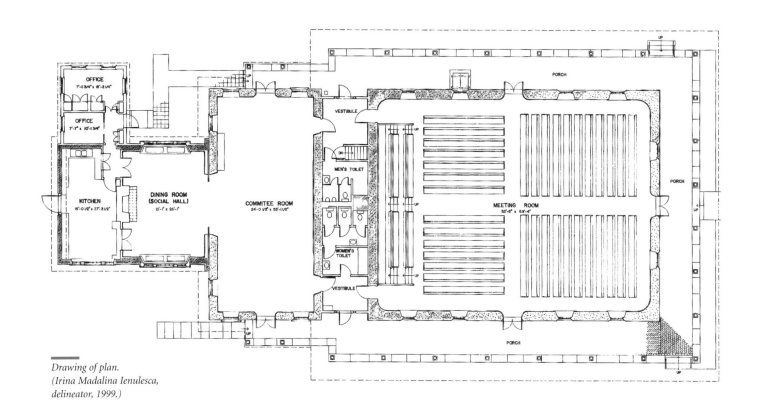

Drawing of plan. (Irina Madalina Ienulesca, delineator, 1999.)

---

[25] The mention in 1908 of a stereopticon (or lantern slide projector) to be used in the committee room suggests that it doubled as a lyceum or lecture hall.

Middletown Preparative Meetinghouse

(built ca. 1702; addition 1790s; remodeled 1888)

Middletown Road, 1 mile N of Pennell Road, Lima vicinity, Delaware County,
Pennsylvania, HABS NO. PA-6655

Detail of facing benches looking northeast. (Jack E. Boucher, photographer, 2001.)

View of the west end which, since 1888, has been the location of the front entry. Note the scalloped shingles and bracketed porch included in the 1888 renovations. (Jack E. Boucher, photographer, 2000.)

Middletown Friends Meeting is among the oldest in what was originally part of Chester Quarter (later Concord). An indulged meeting for worship began in 1686 and was held in the home of John Bowater. In 1690, the Middletown Friends purchased land with the intention of establishing a burying ground and building a meetinghouse. It was shortly thereafter that preparative meeting status was granted by the Chester Monthly Meeting and the earliest section of the meetinghouse was built. Middletown Meetinghouse was begun as early as 1702 as a single-cell, three-bay, central-entry structure typical of the rural meetinghouses of the Delaware Valley during the colonial period.[26] During the 1790s, the building was doubled in size through the addition of a second apartment to better accommodate separate men's and women's business meetings.[27] The resulting two-celled structure was in keeping with the newly established prototype for American Friends meetinghouse design that consisted of a six-bay-long structure with equally sized apartments for men and women, each with its own entryway. While much of the early structure has been obscured by the changes made during the late 19th century, remnants of an earlier period are clearly visible in the attic. These include a barrel-vaulted ceiling, and some of its 18th-century eight-over-eight light sash windows.

In 1888, Middletown Preparative Meetinghouse was significantly altered for the second time in its history in order to conform to changing patterns of meetinghouse development. At that time the meetinghouse was reconfigured. The dual entries located along the west elevation were filled in and a single entry and entrance lobby were created in the gable end, thereby establishing a more church-like appearance and orientation. Likewise, the facing benches were removed from the long, east wall and placed in the opposing gable end. As with meetinghouses such as Little Egg Harbor, this last change reflected a tendency that began in the later 19th century within some Friends meetings to adopt elements of mainstream ecclesiastic architecture. The meetinghouse is still actively being used.

Sectional drawing looking east to show the partition details, structural framing and vaulted ceiling currently located above a dropped ceiling. (Cleary Larkin and Kelly Willard, delineators, 1999.)

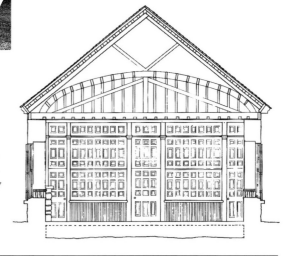

---

[26] The Chester Monthly Meeting minutes, 28 day 7 mo. 1702. For the first time, the minutes on this date note a meeting at the "Middletown Meeting House" rather than at John Bowater's house.

[27] Date based upon accounting for extensive renovations made during that time period, Middletown Preparative Meeting, Treasurers Book, 1791–1815, Friends Historical Library, Swarthmore College, Swarthmore, Pa.

NEW WEST GROVE MEETINGHOUSE (1831; altered 1880s)

State Road, 1 mile W of Rte. 841, West Grove, Chester County, Pennsylvania, HABS No. PA-6665

Open clerk's desk located on the upper tier of the facing benches, looking east. (Jack E. Boucher, photographer, 2001.)

New West Grove Meetinghouse was constructed in 1831 by the Hicksite Friends of West Grove Meeting. It was altered in the 1880s and now serves as a physical manifestation of a significant change in Friends practice. The meetinghouse was built in the typical two-cell, dual-entry form that was conducive to a pattern of meeting whereby men and women sat on separate sides of a partition for both worship and business meetings. When separate business meetings were eliminated at New West Grove in the 1880s, the two original front entries were filled in and the current single, centrally located doorway was installed. Likewise, the now obsolete partition that divided the meetinghouse into separate apartments was taken down. The gradual elimination of separate men's and women's business meetings began in earnest in the 1870s. Although the practice was not officially eliminated within Philadelphia Yearly Meeting until 1923, individual meetings were given the freedom to conduct their meetings as they saw fit. For this reason, there was often a wide discrepancy in the times during which the various meetings chose to adopt changes that had the potential to affect the physical form of their meetinghouses. Some meetings never bothered to alter their meetinghouses to conform to new patterns, underscoring the fact that PYM did not require any building form for Quaker meetinghouses.

Perspective view of the south front and east side facades. (Jack E. Boucher, photographer, 2001.)

Facing benches along the north rear wall and a view through the side entryway, looking northwest. (Jack E. Boucher, photographer, 2001.)

WEST PHILADELPHIA MEETINGHOUSE (1901)

3500 Lancaster Avenue at end of 35th Street, City of Philadelphia, Pennsylvania, HABS No. PA-6664

Perspective view of the north front facade of the meeting-house section. (Joseph Elliott, photographer, 1999).

West Philadelphia Meeting began in 1837 as an indulged meeting under the care of Philadelphia Monthly Meeting. It remained as an indulged meeting for quite some time. Meetings were held in a room within a preexisting structure, the nature of which is not known. It was not until 1851 that a meetinghouse was erected for the use of West Philadelphia Friends, and in 1853 a school opened in the basement of the structure. While the construction of a meetinghouse had been proposed early on, it is likely that the Friends population in this area did not warrant the expenditure. It was not until midcentury that urban development in West Philadelphia was sparked by speculative ventures such as William Hamilton's Hamilton Village—built on a portion of his Woodlands estate. Development in West Philadelphia remained slow for some time due largely to issues of transportation to and from center city. To entice home-buyers, Hamilton made provision for building lots to be donated to various religious denominations, including Friends. It was on this donated lot located at 42nd Street and Powelton Avenue that the Orthodox Friends built a second meetinghouse in West Philadelphia in 1873 (the building is now used as a Presbyterian church). That same year, a separate school building was erected on the site of the 1851 meetinghouse on Lancaster Avenue.

The rise in population among West Philadelphia Friends that necessitated these construction projects reflects both a migration of Friends out of center city and the concurrent move to create suburban neighborhoods. By this time, many Friends of the upper and middle socioeconomic classes left the increasingly congested areas of Center City. While the wealthier Friends chose Germantown or places along the Main Line such as Haverford, middle-class Friends stopped in West Philadelphia. In 1901, the earlier meetinghouse was replaced by the current structure, which represents the first time that a meetinghouse and school were built together as a complex within the domain of Philadelphia Yearly Meeting. After the meeting was laid down, the building was given over for use by the local residents as a community center.

Stairway located in the school portion of building complex, looking north. (Joseph Elliott, photographer, 1999).

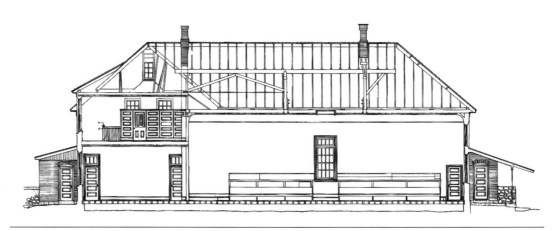

WEST GROVE MEETINGHOUSE (1903)

153 East Harmony Road, West Grove, Chester County, Pennsylvania, HABS NO. PA-6228

Benches in quarterly meeting room, looking southeast. (Jack E. Boucher, photographer, 2001.)

Erected in 1903, West Grove Meetinghouse is an example of a building type that became common within Philadelphia Yearly Meeting during the early 20th century. Friends held an organized meeting for worship at West Grove starting in 1786 and the present building replaced one that had stood on the exact same location since 1787. While the earlier meetinghouse at this site essentially replicated the prototypical two-cell form employed by Friends elsewhere since the third quarter of the 18th century, the 1903 structure represented a design solution being tested at the turn of the century after nearly 100 years of relative uniformity in meetinghouse architecture. Here preparative and quarterly meetings, social gathering, and restroom and kitchen facilities were accommodated in a single construction phase rather than being housed in additions or separate buildings as in years past. In addition, the partition used to separate men's and women's meetings for business was for the first time omitted from the building plans, though joint business meetings did not actually begin at West Grove until 1919. Built to accommodate the Orthodox Western Quarterly Meeting, West Grove arose during a wave of quarterly meetinghouse construction that, by 1911, had also reached Concord, Caln, and Haddonfield Quarters. The innovations apparent in West Grove also surfaced in these buildings to greater or lesser degrees.[28]

West Grove is significant for the continuity as well as the change it embodied. In accordance with traditional Quaker building practice, the structure was designed and constructed by meeting members, and incorporated materials salvaged from the structure it replaced. Framing timbers and the foundation were among the most significant elements of the old meetinghouse to be utilized. Construction of West Grove Meetinghouse was undertaken by skilled craftsmen who were members of the meeting—most notably the builder, Truman Moore, who brought with him many years of experience in the building trades. But in addition to the tremendous contributions of Friend Moore, a "comparatively large amount of gratuitous labor" was forthcoming from other members of meeting.[29] The account book also notes individuals who had personally seen to the acquisition of building materials and other parts, again speaking to the communal nature of the building process. The meetinghouse is still actively used.

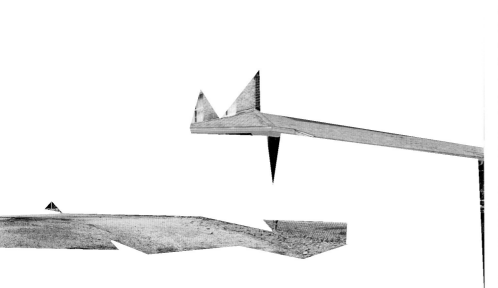

Perspective view of the south front and east side facades, looking northwest. (Jack E. Boucher, photographer, 2001.)

Sectional drawing looking north. Note the somewhat unusual framing of the roof that resulted from the reuse of building materials from the former meetinghouse. The preparative meeting room is to the left side and the quarterly meeting room is to the right. (H. Christie Barnard, delineator, 1997.)

---

[28] Aaron Wunsch, et al. "West Grove Friends Meeting House," National Park Service, Historic American Buildings Survey, HABS NO. PA-6228, Summer 1997, 1.

[29] West Grove Preparative Meeting, Report of the Building Committee, 29 day 11 mo. 1904, 3.

Westtown Meetinghouse (1929)

On campus of Westtown School, Westtown, Chester County, Pennsylvania, HABS No. PA-6686

North front and west end. (Jack E. Boucher, photographer, 2002.)

An indulged meeting for worship was established for the accommodation of students and teachers on the campus of Westtown Friends Boarding School by Philadelphia Yearly Meeting in 1799. From that time until 1929, meetings were held in a room within the main school building. In 1920, the meeting became a monthly meeting under the care of Concord Quarterly Meeting and was no longer used exclusively by the school population. In 1929 funding provided by Arthur and Emma Foster Perry made possible the construction of the current meetinghouse. Westtown Friends Meetinghouse was designed by Quaker architect Walter Price in the doubled form that had once been considered a prototype of meetinghouse design. The six-bay doubled form had long since fallen out of favor due largely to such changes in Quaker practice as joint business meetings that called for the elimination of its key interior design feature: dual apartments separated by a retractable partition. Likely motivated by the Colonial Revival movement in American architecture, Walter Price made a study of old forms before developing the design of this meetinghouse, as well as the design of other similar meetinghouses in Washington, D.C., and in Montclair, New Jersey. Perhaps equally as significant is the fact that the meetinghouse *was* architect-designed. Few meetinghouse designs in the Delaware Valley can be attributed to an architect. Hence, the development of Westtown marks a significant shift in building practice from the days in which meetinghouses were planned and constructed by members of the meeting to the commissioning of professionals.

Facing benches with the sounding board above, looking west. (Jack E. Boucher, photographer, 2002.))

CHESTNUT HILL MEETINGHOUSE (1931)

100 E. Mermaid Lane, Philadelphia, Pennsylvania, HABS No. PA-6688

Entry pavilion at the northwest front facade. (Jack E. Boucher, photographer, 2000.)

W hen built in 1931, Chestnut Hill Meetinghouse was innovative in ways indicative of the modern era in Friends history. Its design reflects the changes that occurred in Quaker faith and practice during the late 19th and early 20th centuries. Chestnut Hill Meetinghouse was designed by architect Joseph Linden Heacock, in concert with meeting members. It received an addition in 1964 that resulted in its current sprawling, single-story configuration. Chestnut Hill was the first meetinghouse in the region to be built without a facing bench. Its construction, therefore, marks the exclusion from modern designs of many of the once-essential elements of meetinghouses. The facing benches, from which the ministers, elders, and overseers presided over the meetings, were eliminated along with its occupants' strict oversight. And the benches that once faced them are arranged in-the-round, further disregarding any hierarchy among members. The focus traditionally provided by the facing benches was substituted by a fireplace. Likewise, the removal of the retractable wood partition traditionally used to separate men and women during their business meetings is reflective of the modern practice of holding a joint business meeting. Like West Grove Meetinghouse, Chestnut Hill's current plan is also expressive of the trend towards providing for a multipurpose facility.

View of meeting room looking southwest. Note the fireplace hearth that replaces the traditional facing benches. (Jack E. Boucher, photographer, 2000.)

Chestnut Hill Meeting is significant as the first to be formed as a "united meeting" following the schism that divided Friends into Orthodox and Hicksite factions in 1827. The meeting began in 1924 with members originating from both Hicksite and Orthodox meetings. However, it was not until 1933 that Chestnut Hill Meeting was recognized as a united meeting by the authority of Abington Quarterly Meeting, under the care of yearly meeting at Arch Street. This occurred in advance of the reunion of the Hicksite and Orthodox groups in 1955. The interest in forming a united meeting is credited to the involvement by many of Chestnut Hill Meeting's founding members in the newly formed American Friends Service Committe (AFSC). Through the AFSC involvement in civilian aid and post-war reconstruction projects, Friends helped to mitigate the effects of the world wars while demonstrating Quaker adherence to the peace testimony. Participation in AFSC came from both Hicksite and Orthodox camps and is therefore believed to have helped reunite the two yearly meetings.

SOUTHAMPTON MEETINGHOUSE (1969)

710 Gravel Hill Road at Street Road, Southampton, Bucks County, Pennsylvania,
HABS NO. PA-6656

Detail of principal entry located towards the (south) front of the west side facade. Note the clerestory roof and cinder block construction. (Jack E. Boucher, photographer, 2000.)

Southampton Meeting began in 1941 when a group of local Friends began to meet informally in one another's homes. In 1947, under the care of the Buckingham Monthly Meeting, Southampton Meeting was officially designated a united meeting, not recognizing the distinctions that still existed between Hicksite and Orthodox contingents. In 1949 it began meeting in a former schoolhouse which it later purchased in 1960. Many of its members were previously members of meetings located in Philadelphia who were desirous of creating a multicultural suburban enclave outside the city. In so doing, Friends formed a cooperative community known as Bryn Gweled Homesteads, located across the road from the meeting site. In 1967 the State Highway Administration announced plans to widen Street Road, which would necessitate the demolition of the former schoolhouse. Friends then looked to the construction of a meetinghouse on the same property. Built in 1969–1970, Southampton is among the most recently constructed Friends meetinghouses in the Delaware Valley. Its contemporary design reflects a break in tradition with regard to both exterior appearance and interior plan. As with Chestnut Hill, changes in Quaker thought and practice that occurred during the late 19th and early 20th centuries were manifested in the design of modern meetinghouses such as this one. The facing benches were eliminated from Southampton and the general benches are arranged in a semicircle so that "no Friends are set apart by a facing bench."[30] The focus once provided by the facing benches was replaced by a large picture window that looks out onto the woods that surround the meetinghouse. Southampton is also missing the partition that traditionally divided meetinghouses into separate rooms. Instead, the meeting room forms a large open space designed for use as a multi-purpose facility. Like many 20th-century meetinghouses, Southampton provides space for the larger functions of the meeting and includes a kitchen, library, and restrooms.

Interior view of meeting room with benches positioned in-the-round and a picture window with a view to the woods in the location traditionally occupied by the facing benches. (Jack E. Boucher, photographer, 2000.)

Southampton Meetinghouse was designed by Quaker architect Bert Klett, and was erected by contractor E. Allen Reeves. It blends Quaker simplicity with modern architecture. Although guided by these professionals, the meeting members took an active role in the design and execution of the meetinghouse as is indicative of Quaker practice. The initial concern of many members of the meeting that focusing on a large building project would have a "deadening effect" upon the meeting and detract from "basic Quaker concerns and the urgent problems of our day," was eventually overcome.[31] In keeping with the Friends focus on people rather than buildings, the intention of the open house held on May 24, 1970, was to celebrate not the completed meetinghouse but the renewed commitment to their faith represented by its construction.

For the purposes of the HABS study, this modern structure marks the end of the continuum in the evolution of meetinghouse design in the Delaware Valley.

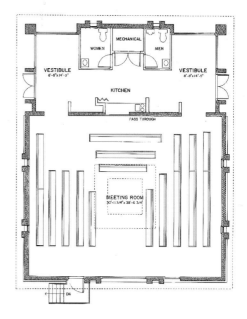

Drawing of plan. (John P. White and Kelly Willard, delineators, 1999.)

---

[30] Helen N. Schantz, "A Rededication of Our Lives," *Friends Journal*, Vol.16 No. 15 (September 1970), 469.
[31] Ibid.

FRIENDS MEETINGHOUSES OF THE DELAWARE VALLEY

As Surveyed by the Historic American Buildings Survey (HABS)

Pennsylvania

Abington (1786/1797)
Abington Orthodox/Little Abington (1836)
Arch Street (Philadelphia Yearly Meeting (1804-1811)
Bart (1825)
Birmingham (1763/1818)**
Birmingham Orthodox (1845); now a residence
Bradford-Marshallton (1767)***
Bristol (1713/1756)
Buckingham (1768)*
Buckingham Orthodox (1830); now a firehouse
Byberry (1808)
Caln (1726/1784/1801)*
Caln Orthodox, Coatesville (1905); now used commerically
Catawissa (1794)
Cheltenham (1958)
Chester (1829)
Chestnut Hill (1931)
Chichester (1769)*
Concord (1728/1788)
Concord Orthodox (1834); now a community center
Darby (1805)
Derry/Doe Run (1883); now a residence
Downingtown (1806)*
Doylestown (1836)
Exeter (1759)**
Falls (1728); now apartments
Falls (1789); now the William Penn Center
Falls Orthodox (1841)
Fairhill (1884); now St. Mark Outreach Baptist Church
Fallowfield (1801)
Frankford Preparative (1775-1776) (now Unity Meeting, Frankford)*
Frankford Orthodox (1833/1865)
Free Quaker (1783)**
George School (1974) rebuilt using remnants of Twelveth Street Meetinghouse (1812)
Germantown (1868-1869)*
Goshen (1855)
Goshen Orthodox (1849); now a Grange Hall and daycare center
Gwynedd (1824)
Gwynedd Orthodox (1830); now a residence
Gwynedd @ Norristown (1890); now Faith Bible Church
(Old) Haverford (1701/1800)
Haverford Orthodox (1834)
Homeville (1839)
Horsham (1803)
Horsham Orthodox (1890); now a residence
(Old) Kennett (ca. 1731)***
Kennett Square (1958)
Lampeter/Leacock (1790)
Lancaster (1759)
Lansdowne (1903); now Apostolic Faith House of Prayer
Lansdowne Orthodox (1831)
London Britian (1834)***
London Grove (1818)***

London Grove Orthodox (1834); now a residence
Longwood/Progressive (1854); now a visitor information center
Maiden Creek (1759)
Maiden Creek Orthodox (1853); now a residence
Makefield (1752/1851)
Marlborough (1801)***
Media-Providence (1875/1885)
Merion (ca. 1695-1714)*
Middletown, Bucks County (1793)
Middletown Preparative, Delaware County (ca. 1702/1797/1888)*
Middletown Orthodox, Delaware County (1835)
Millville (1846)**
New Garden (1743/1790)
New Garden Orthodox (1827); now a residence
Norristown (1852)
Newtown (1817)
Newtown Square (1791)***
New West Grove (1831)
Parkersville (1830)
Pennsgrove (1833)
Plumstead (1752/1876)
Plymouth (ca. 1708/ca. 1790s)
Plymouth Orthodox (1828); a residence for many years but now used for school classrooms
Powelton/West Philadelphia Orthodox (1878), now the Lombard Central Presbyterian Church
Providence (1814-1815)
Race Street/Hicksite Yearly Meetinghouse (1857-1858)
Radnor (1718/1780s)*
Reading (1868)**
Richland/Quakertown (1862)
Roaring Creek (1798)
Romansville (1846)**
Sadsbury (1747)*
Sadsbury/Christiana (1902); now a Mennonite Church
Schuylkill (1807/1816)
Solebury (1806)
Southampton (1969)*
Springfield (1851)
Swarthmore (1881/1901)
Unami (1974)
Unionville (1845); now a Grange Hall
Upper Dublin (1814)
Upper Providence (1828)
Uwchlan (1756); now a community center
Valley (1871)
West Chester (1810/1868)
Westtown (1929)
West Grove (1903)*
West Grove Hicksite (1901); now a church
Willistown (1798)
West Philadelphia (1901) —now a community arts center
Wrightstown (1789)
Yardley (1956)

New Jersey

Arney's Mount (1775)*
Atlantic City (1926-1927); now the lobby of the Quality Inn
Barnegat (1851)**
Bordentown (1740)**; now bank offices
Burlington (1784)
Copany/Springfield (1775); now a residence
Cropwell (1809)
Crosswicks/Chesterfield (1773)**
Crosswicks/Chesterfield Orthodox (1854); now the Chesterfeild Township Historical Society
Easton (1811); now the Easton Union Church
Eavesham/Mt. Laurel (1760/1798)**
Haddonfield (1851); now the Acme grocery
Haddonfield Orthodox (1851)
Hancock's Bridge/Alloways Creek (1756/1784)
Greenwich (1771)**
Greenwich Hicksite (1857)***
Little Egg Harbor (1863)*
Mansfield/Upper Springfield (1812)
Medford (1842); for sale at time of survey
Medford Orthodox (1812)
Mickletown/Upper Greenwich (1799)
Moorestown (1802)
Moorestown Orthodox (1897); now the Moorestown Friends School gymnasium
Mt. Holly (1775/1850)
Mullica Hill/Woolwich (1808)
Newton (1828/1885)
Plainfield (1788)**
Quakertown (1862)
Rancocas (1772)**
Randolph/Medham (1758)**
Salem (1772)**
Salem Orthodox (1837); now law offices
Seaville (1763/1981)**
Shrewsbury (1816)••
Squan (1884)**
Stony Brook (1726/1760)••
Trenton (1739/1872/1896)
Trenton Orthodox (1855); now offices, Mercer Street Friends Center
(Old) Upper Springfield (1727); now a residence
Westfield (1859); now a daycare center
(new) Westfield (1963)
Woodbury (1715/1783)**
Woodstown (1785)

Delaware:

Camden (1805)**
Centre (1796)**
Hockessin (1738)**
Mill Creek (1840-41)**
Stanton (1873); now dentist offices
Wilmington (1815-17)**
Odessa/Appoquinimink (1785)**

NOTE: Those in **bold** have been documented with large-format photographs and written history, and those also indicated by * include measured drawings. Meetinghouses previously recorded by HABS are indicated by **. Meetinghouses that were drawn by students from the University of Delaware, under the direction of Professor Bernard Herman, and donated to HABS are indicated by ***.

Selected References

The following are basic sources on Quakers and Quaker architecture, with special attention to Philadelphia Yearly Meeting. The records of Philadelphia Yearly Meeting and its local meetings are in the joint custody of Friends Historical Library at Swarthmore College and at the Quaker Collection, Magill Library, Haverford College. In addition, these institutions hold archival and manuscript collections and extensive book, periodical, and visual holdings documenting the Society of Friends. The catalogs of both repositories can be searched online through the TRIPOD system.

Barbour, Hugh and J. William Frost. *The Quakers.* Richmond, Indiana: Friends United Press, 1994.

Bauman, Richard. *For the Reputation of Truth; Politics, Religion, and Conflict among the Pennsylvania Quakers, 1750–1800.* Baltimore: John Hopkins University Press, 1971.

Benjamin, Philip S. *The Philadelphia Quakers in the Industrial Age, 1865–1910.* Philadelphia: Temple University Press, 1976.

Bonner, Ruth E. *Quaker Ways: Pictures of Quaker Meeting Houses in Current Middle-Atlantic America.* Kutztown, PA: Kutztown Publishing, 1978.

Brinton, Howard H. *Friends For 300 Years: The History and Beliefs of the Society of Friends Since George Fox Started the Quaker Movement.* Wallingford, PA: Pendle Hill Publications, 1952.

Bronner, Edwin B. "Quaker Landmarks in Early Philadelphia." *American Philosophical Society,* Vol. 43, Pt. 1(1953): 210-16.

Brown, Francis G. *Old Caln Meeting House: Its Story.* Glenmoore, Pa: Glenmoore Corporation, 2001.

_____. *Downingtown Friends Meeting: An Early History of Quakers in the Great Valley.* Glenmoore,Pa: Glenmoore Corporation, 1999.

Butler, David M. *Quaker Meeting Houses of the Lake Counties.* Friends Historical Society, 1978.

_____. "Quaker Meeting Houses in America and England: Impressions and Comparisons." *Quaker History,* vol. 79, no. 2 (Fall 1990): 93–104.

_____. "The Making of Meeting Houses." *Friends Quarterly* (July 1980): 316–24.

_____. *The Quaker Meeting Houses of Britain.* London: Friends Historical Society, 1999. 2 vol.

Clarkson, Thomas. *A Portraiture of Quakerism.* 2d American ed. Philadelphia: James P. Parke, 1808.

Eckert, Jack. *Guide to the Records of Philadelphia Yearly Meeting.* Philadelphia: Records Committee of the Philadelphia Yearly Meeting, 1989.

Frost, J. William, and John M. Moore, eds. *Seeking the Light: Essays in Quaker History in Honor of Edwin B. Bronner.* Haverford, Pa.: Friends Historical Association, 1986.

Frost, J. William. *The Quaker Family in Colonial America.* New York: St. Martin's Press, 1973.

Hinshaw, Seth Beeson. "The Evolution of Quaker Meeting Houses in North America, 1670–2000." M.S. Thesis, University of Pennsylvania, 2001.

Jones, Rufus M. *The Quakers in the American Colonies.* New York: The Norton Library, W.W. Norton & Company, 1966.

Lidbetter, Hubert. *The Friends Meeting House,* 3rd ed. York: William Sessions, 1995.

_____. "Quaker Meeting Houses, 1670–1850." *Architectural Review* (London) 99 (1946): 99–116.

Lippincott, Horace Mather. *Meeting Houses and a Little Humor.* Jenkintown,Pa.: Old York Road Publishing Co., 1952.

Marietta, Jack. *The Reformation of American Quakerism, 1748–1783.* Philadelphia: University of Pennsylvania Press, 1984.

Matlack, T. Chalkley. *Brief Historical Sketches Concerning Friends' Meetings of the Past and Present with Special Reference to Philadelphia Yearly Meeting,* (the original volumes are located at The Quaker Collection, Haverford College Library; copy available at Friends Historical Library), 1938.

Moore, John M. *Friends in the Delaware Valley: Philadelphia Yearly Meeting, 1681–1981.* Haverford, Pa.: Friends Historical Association, 1981.

Pennsylvania Historical Survey, Division of Community Service Programs, Work Projects Administration. *Inventory of Church Archives, Society of Friends in Pennsylvania.* Philadelphia: Friends Historical Association, 1941.

Russell, Elbert. *The History of Quakerism.* New York: The MacMillan Company, 1942.

Tolles, Frederick B. *Quakers and the Atlantic Culture.* New York: Macmillian Co., 1960.

Tvaryanas, Damon. "The New Jersey Quaker Meeting House: A Typology and Inventory," M.S. Thesis, University of Pennsylvania, 1993.

Wilson, Robert H. *Philadelphia Quakers, 1681–1981.* Philadelphia: Philadelphia Yearly Meeting, 1981.

Photography by Jack E. Boucher, HABS photographer, and Joseph Elliott for HABS; photographic printing by HABS photographer James Rosenthal. The catalog text was written by Catherine C. Lavoie, HABS Historian; with essays by Christopher Densmore and Catherine C. Lavoie. Robert Dockhorn served as copy editor. The catalog was designed by Mark Willie, Willie•Fetchko Graphic Design.

The documentation was undertaken 1996–2001 by the Historic American Buildings Survey (HABS) of the National Park Service, E. Blaine Cliver, Chief of HABS/HAER; Paul Dolinsky, Chief of HABS. Funding was provided by a Congressional appropriation for Southeastern Pennsylvania, and a grant from the William Penn Foundation. The project was planned and administered by HABS historians Catherine C. Lavoie and Aaron V. Wunsch, and HABS architect Robert R. Arzola. The field survey was conducted by Catherine C. Lavoie and Aaron V. Wunsch. The historical reports were written by Catherine C. Lavoie, Virginia Price, and Aaron V. Wunsch. Measured drawings were produced by field teams working under the direction of Robert Arzola in 1997 and 1999, including: Aaron Wunsch, Field Supervisor; Roger S. Miller, Architect, & technicians: H. Christie Barnard, Pamela Howell, Kevin J. Lam, Adam Maksay (US ICOMOS); John P. White, Architect, & technicians: Cleary Larkin, James McGrath, Jr., Elaine Schweitzer, Kelly Willard, Irina Madalina Ienulescu (US ICOMOS).

Special thanks for their assistance goes to: the clerks, caretakers, and members of the participant meetings; Peggy Morscheck, Director, Quaker Information Center; Helen File, Director, Arch Street Meeting-house; Patricia O'Donnell, Susanna K. Morikawa, and Charlotte Blanford, archivists; Mary Ellen Chijioke (former curator) and Christopher Densmore, Curator, Friends Historical Library of Swarthmore College; Diana F. Peterson, Joelle Bertole, and Elisabeth Potts Brown, archivists, and Emma Lapsansky, Curator, Quaker Collection, Haverford College; and the PYM Publications Service Group, Jim Harrington, Odie LeFever, and Paul Rodebaugh.